PRAISE FOR *FEEDBACK*

'Best of the Best' is an apt series title for a gem of a book that bridges that often neglected gap between theory and practical application. I fully expect feedback from my students that I am a better teacher as a result of reading it!

The book provides a much needed one-stop shop for a brilliant range of leading educationalists to share their wisdom. For the busy teacher, this 'lazy' approach is hard to beat!

A cracking book bursting with accessible ideas on feedback from education's leading lights. What's more, the ideas are all rooted in research, wisdom and the often forgotten ingredient to make them classroom friendly: common sense.

Jim Smith, Head of School, Clevedon School and author of *The Lazy Teacher's Handbook*

This short guide offers a great mix of expert ideas, theoretical explanations and practical applications for the classroom. If you're looking for the most up-to-date advice on feedback, or if you want to read more widely around an important subject, then this is the book for you.

Sue Cowley, teacher and author of *The Artful Educator*

Feedback, in the Best of the Best series, makes a significant contribution to the literature on this essential aspect of teaching. The editors have collated succinct summaries from top thought leaders on the subject: from Dylan Wiliam, Ron Berger, Barry Hymer and Shirley Clarke to Seth Godin. Each chapter contains a distillation of their position on feedback and an exploration of the importance of thinking carefully about how we go about giving and receiving it. The practical suggestions are particularly useful as ways of consolidating high quality practice in the classroom. Above all, this book cuts through the nonsense of cheap praise and reaches to the heart of the matter. An essential read.

**Mary Myatt, education adviser, speaker
and author of *Hopeful Schools***

An easily digestible and accessible guide to feedback, compiled from contributions by the world's leading experts in teaching and learning. The magic gold dust is the practical and realistic strategies, offered after each chapter, about how to implement these theories directly in the classroom. I challenge any teacher, whether at the start of their career or nearing the end, not to find innovative ways to change the way they deliver and receive feedback!

**Rebecca Poorhady, Learning and Development Organiser,
Midlands region, Association of Teachers and Lecturers**

The future depends on people being capable of managing themselves; of taking ownership of their own challenges. To do that, they will need to understand their strengths and weaknesses with objectivity and constructive thinking. In many ways, how we structure and develop feedback for our students, in order to help them develop that level of autonomy, has never been more important. This book is a gold mine of thinking, ideas and practical solutions to help us.

Dr Richard Gerver, expert in leadership, change and success

Teaching is exciting if we make it exciting by providing children with the opportunity to meet their own destination. The ideas and concepts within this book allow for this, and the opening of minds and doors, to happen!

Michelle Slymn, Principal, All Saints National Academy

FEEDBACK

BEST OF THE BEST
PRACTICAL CLASSROOM GUIDES

FEEDBACK

ISABELLA WALLACE AND LEAH KIRKMAN

Crown House Publishing Limited
www.crownhouse.co.uk

First published by

Crown House Publishing Ltd
Crown Buildings, Bancyfelin, Carmarthen, Wales, SA33 5ND, UK
www.crownhouse.co.uk

and

Crown House Publishing Company LLC
PO Box 2223, Williston, VT 05495
www.crownhousepublishing.com

First published 2017

British Library Cataloguing-in-Publication Data
A catalogue entry for this book is available from the British Library.

Print ISBN 978-178583187-4
Mobi ISBN 978-178583242-0
ePub ISBN 978-178583243-7
ePDF ISBN 978-178583244-4

LCCN 2017940082

Printed and bound in the UK by
Gomer Press, Llandysul, Ceredigion

PREFACE

When some of us started teaching many moons ago, our initial preparatory training and the subsequent professional development we received didn't really expose us to a wealth of educational thinkers, theorists or researchers. There were the staples – perhaps a pinch of Piaget here or a dusting of Dewey there ... But times are changing. Today – right now – we are witnessing the dawn of a very different informational landscape. Important, knowledgeable voices in education ring out from all directions. Not simply political ones, but the voices of experts and practitioners who have devoted significant time in their lives to the education of young people or examining the issues that surround it.

This is a wonderful development. But teachers are notoriously busy. Sometimes those of us working in education are *so* busy that being faced with such an array of diverse opinions and theories can feel overwhelming rather than helpful. It can be hard to see how we might apply ideas to our own schools and classrooms, our own year groups or subjects.

The purpose of the 'Best of the Best' series is to bring together – for the first time – the most influential voices in one accessible format. A compendium of the most useful advice from the most celebrated educationalists. Each title in the series focuses on a different all-important theme and features a comprehensive collection of brief and accessible contributions from the most eminent names in education internationally. In these books you have it straight from the horse's mouth. But that's not all: in close liaison with those experts, we have developed practical, realistic, cross-curricular and cross-phase ways to make the most of these important insights *in the classroom*.

We've translated theory into practice for you, and every edition in the series is written for teachers, by teachers. Of course, if a particular concept takes your fancy and you have time to delve a little deeper, all of our experts have pointed you in the right direction for further reading. And all of a sudden the continuing professional development (CPD) voyage seems a little less overwhelming. Contented sigh.

To top it all off, the wonderful Teacher Development Trust has outlined a collaborative group approach for teachers to read the book together and try out the ideas, as well as providing helpful guidance to school leaders on how to set up CPD around the book's theme for maximum impact.

Have a breathtaking adventure discovering the best tips from the best people, and don't forget to look out for other titles in the collection!

Isabella Wallace and Leah Kirkman

ACKNOWLEDGEMENTS

Once again, we want to thank the unique collection of busy experts who have pooled their wisdom, research and insight into this second book in the 'Best of the Best' series.

Thank you, too, to the Crown House team who continue to help us bring together the best authorities on education from all over the world. We know it's no mean feat!

Huge thanks to the pupils who have given us feedback on our own teaching strategies over the years and helped us to refine and develop them for maximum impact on learning. (And it would be rude not to mention the coffee shop where so many of the practical strategies for this book have been written up. You let us sit there, drinking endless tea and using your Wi-Fi, and you still give us smiley service!)

We are again very grateful to David Weston and the Teacher Development Trust for collaborating with us to review the ideas and affix their guidance to the series, and to Professor Sue Wallace, who has once again provided invaluable guidance in drawing ideas together.

Finally, we want to say a big thank you to the thousands of teachers we've worked with who have given us feedback – and taken it too. It is your 'feedback' that matters most of all.

CONTENTS

INTRODUCTION

The term 'feedback' is a relative newcomer to the English lexicon. It was coined in the early 20th century during the development of broadcasting technology to describe the sort of disruptive noise you will almost certainly have heard at some time or another when your favourite guitar player has wandered too close to the amplifier. Later, it was adopted by communication theorists who gave it a much more positive spin, using it as the term for an incoming response to an outgoing message – a signal that tells us the communication has been received. Most familiar to us now in an educational context, its meaning has further evolved and diversified.

Feedback is often cited as one of the most powerful tools for enhancing learning. And in the classroom it can be understood and implemented in a whole range of ways, as our contributors – the best of the best – demonstrate in the following pages. But although they each provide their own unique take on the importance of feedback to teaching and learning, they are unanimous in emphasising the paramount importance of feedback as clear *communication* – the context in which our current understanding of the word originated.

Dylan Wiliam, for example, points out the importance of formative assessment as a means of enabling the teacher to make evidence-based decisions about each student's needs, and stresses the importance of this source of feedback as a way of gaining insight into what students are getting out of the teaching process. Similarly, Mike Gershon, who makes the link to communication theory quite explicit with his diagram of the 'feedback loop', illustrates the point that feedback is not a one-off response but a continuing process or dialogue. However, for a student to respond effectively and constructively to the feedback they are given by the teacher, they must be allowed time in which to reflect on it and implement it. Their response is a continuation of the feedback loop – the two-way communication conducted over time. This same point about feedback being a two-way process is made by Andy Griffith, who also employs the language of communication theory when he argues that, for the teacher, feedback is something we should be able to both give and receive. He explores this idea in the light of the question: how can we encourage our students to be more open to feedback? The answer, he suggests, lies in the willingness of the teacher to model this openness themselves by inviting and acting on student feedback in order to improve the effectiveness of their own practice.

This idea of feedback from students to teachers – a reversal of our usual assumptions about the direction of flow – is also taken up by Mick Waters, who suggests formalising this process by inviting students to award points to teachers based on the teacher's effectiveness in helping the student to learn. Shirley Clarke, too, argues that it is feedback from learners to teachers which constitutes the most significant and productive means of improving students' learning experience and supporting their learning. This application of feedback, as an important opportunity for learning and improvement for teachers as well as their students, is a point also made by Jackie Beere, whose contribution focuses on how best to encourage a positive response to feedback. She advocates introducing the idea of 'thinking on purpose' – the practice of reflecting on feedback in order to be able to act on it appropriately and productively. To this end, she points out the advantages – whether you are a teacher or a student – of reframing critical feedback as something positive rather than negative; as a valuable opportunity to learn and improve. Indeed, this emphasis on feedback as a trigger for action is one also shared by Andy Griffith, Mike Gershon and several others.

Other contributors give us a different perspective, focusing instead on what constitutes the most useful and effective feedback. For example, Art Costa and Robert Garmston challenge the notion that feedback should be about giving praise. Writing in the context of feedback on teacher performance, they argue that praise can actually be counterproductive, since it encourages dependency on the assessor rather than developing a capacity for reflection in the person being assessed. A more useful and productive form of feedback, they argue, is to use what they term 'data description' – describing what you see. Barry Hymer, in his contribution, makes the same point. Praise and reward can, he tells us, be detrimental to intrinsic motivation. If a student relies for motivation on praise from the teacher, they won't learn to motivate themselves and develop a love of learning for its own sake. Their engagement with learning will always be dependent on the promise of a prize or external reward. Like Costa and Garmston, Hymer argues that simple praise and reward only serve to keep the teacher in control, and thereby rob the student of self-efficacy. Instead, teachers should aim to give acknowledgement, encouragement and feedback that is both detailed and specific, a point also made by Seth Godin, who suggests that feedback should offer an analysis rather than simply an opinion: 'This worked because ...' rather than 'I liked this.' Godin makes the further point that timing is crucial to ensuring that the feedback you give will be effective in improving performance, because if it is given too early or too late the student (or indeed teacher) will not be in a position to act on it.

The argument for analytical and specific feedback is taken up by Ron Berger and Diana Laufenberg, who both argue for the importance of giving feedback referenced to clear criteria. Their practical approaches to this differ, however. Laufenberg places an emphasis on the importance of making time to give detailed, face-to-face feedback against the assessment criteria to each individual student. This face-to-face delivery, she argues, is both more effective and more encouraging than written feedback. Berger, on the other hand, lays no particular emphasis on giving feedback face to face, but argues for the importance of giving individual, descriptive feedback on specific aspects of student work or performance and of avoiding general, holistic statements such as 'good work'.

On the other hand, Phil Beadle argues that praise should be considered a very important element when giving feedback. Using the analogy of a coach encouraging a football team, he illustrates the way in which praise has the power to motivate in the immediate moment in a way that analytical criticism does not. However, praise should, he tells us, always be followed by advice on how to do even better. Geoff Petty, too, cites praise as one of the key factors for effective learning which has emerged from meta studies of evidence-based research, together with clearly understood goals and the will to improve. And Taylor Mali, writing in the context of giving feedback to parents on a child's performance and attainment, also makes a case for giving positive feedback, suggesting that negative feedback will be less likely to lead to improvement than if the teacher accentuates what is praiseworthy while highlighting the room for development within that positive context. Nevertheless, more important even than feedback, Mali argues, is what he refers to as 'feedfront' – giving clear instructions and setting clear goals before a task even begins. In this respect he is in agreement with Ron Berger, Diana Laufenberg and others who stress the need for feedback to be linked to clear, previously stated criteria.

Although several contributors warn against giving generalised and non-specific praise, this does not discount, of course, the need for a positive approach with an emphasis on demonstrating kindness, encouragement and helpfulness in the giving of feedback – whatever that feedback may be. Seth Godin, for example, reminds us to 'say something nice' if we can. Similarly,

Ron Berger tells us that we must be 'kind' when feeding back on work, whatever it is that must be said. And Art Costa and Robert Garmston, who take a strong position against feedback that is simply evaluative, stress at the same time the need to establish a sense of trust if the feedback we give is to be accepted as meaningful and constructive.

Some of the contributors provide advice about very specific approaches. Paul Dix, for example, gives a detailed account of the use of student wristbands on which they can record the useful feedback they have been given. This is a way of encouraging them to take ownership – literally – of their own progress and ongoing targets for learning. Bill Lucas, too, in arguing that we must give students the opportunity and choice to accept or reject the feedback advice that we offer them, is also raising the issue of students taking ownership, albeit in a less material sense. A further example of a contributor who gives us some insight into the practical implications of her approach is Diana Laufenberg, who explains how she makes time for one-to-one feedback by planning work that the rest of the class can absorb themselves in while she speaks to each individual.

From these contributions, each unique and enlightening in its own right, a number of key themes emerge. One of these is the need to get the balance right between praise and constructive critique by keeping feedback specific, detailed and firmly referenced to clearly explained criteria. Another is that these same principles should be applied whether the feedback is from teacher to student, teacher to colleague, student to teacher or student to student. Response to feedback, too, emerges as a theme: the need to give students the time to reflect on it, to question it, to act on it. And, of course, we have a theme which relates to the manner in which feedback should be given: kindly, constructively, in a timely way and in an atmosphere of trust. Above all, perhaps, these contributors are united in the view that what effective feedback is primarily about is clear, constructive and specific communication.

In what follows, you will find the detail of what each expert has to say in their own distinctive voice. For each of these important insights, you will find a number of ways to practically implement the experts' ideas in your own classroom or even across your whole school. Some experts have provided their own strategies, and everything that is from the experts' own voices appears in white text on a black background. Looking for some ways to facilitate peer feedback without witnessing comments like, 'Your story is awesome' or 'Include more words'? Desperate to stop that sensitive student from taking personal offence every time you offer constructive feedback? Interested in rediscovering your social life by acquiring new ways to make written feedback less time consuming? Read on to see what some of the greatest names in education have to say about feedback and explore a host of practical strategies that will enable you to ensure that feedback – in *your* classroom – is truly the powerfully transformative tool it has the potential to be.

PROFESSOR DYLAN WILIAM is Emeritus Professor of Educational Assessment at University College London. After seven years of teaching in London schools, he joined Chelsea College, which later became part of King's College London. In a varied career, he has trained teachers, managed a large-scale testing programme and served a number of roles in university administration. He has written over 300 books, articles and chapters, many with his long-time colleague Paul Black. His most recent books are *Embedding Formative Assessment: Practical Techniques for K-12 Classrooms* (with Siobhán Leahy, 2015) and *Leadership for Teacher Learning* (2016).

CHAPTER 1

FORMATIVE ASSESSMENT:
THE BRIDGE BETWEEN TEACHING AND LEARNING

PROFESSOR DYLAN WILIAM

Formative assessment is at the heart of good teaching because of one principle about learning and one uncomfortable fact about the world. The principle is that *good teaching starts from where learners are, rather than where we would like them to be*. The uncomfortable fact about the world is that *students do not learn what we teach*. Put these two things together and the need for formative assessment is clear. We need to find out what our students have learned before we teach them anything else.

Of course, the fact that students know something today does not mean they will know it in six weeks' time – as Paul Kirschner reminds us, learning is a change in long-term memory (Kirschner et al., 2006). But if they don't know something today, it is highly unlikely they will know it in six weeks' time. Formative assessment is based on the simple idea that it is better to know what is going on in the heads of our students than not.

Some people argue that the term 'formative assessment' is unhelpful – this is, after all, just good teaching. But the use of the word 'assessment' draws attention to the quality of evidence the teacher has for the decisions that need to be taken. If you are only getting answers to your questions from confident students, you can't possibly make decisions that reflect the learning needs of the whole class. And, of course, once you find out what your students have learned, you need to provide feedback to the students that helps them to move their learning forward, rather than just telling them what's wrong with their existing work. After all, the purpose of feedback is to improve the student, not the work they have just done.

And this means a fundamental shift in perspective, from looking at what the teacher is putting into the process to what the students are getting out of it. As one teacher said, it's all about making the students' voices louder and the teacher's hearing better.

FURTHER READING

Black, Paul, Harrison, Chris, Lee, Clara, Marshall, Bethan and Wiliam, Dylan (2003). *Assessment for Learning: Putting It Into Practice* (Buckingham: Open University Press).

Kirschner, Paul A., Sweller, John and Clark, Richard E. (2006). Why Minimal Guidance During Instruction Does Not Work: An Analysis of the Failure of Constructivist, Discovery, Problem-Based, Experiential, and Inquiry-Based Teaching, *Educational Psychologist* 41(2): 75–86.

Wiliam, Dylan (2011). *Embedded Formative Assessment* (Bloomington, IN: Solution Tree).

Wiliam, Dylan (2016). *Leadership for Teacher Learning: Creating a Culture Where All Teachers Improve So That All Learners Succeed* (West Palm Beach, FL: Learning Sciences International).

Wiliam, Dylan and Leahy, Siobhán (2015). *Embedding Formative Assessment: Practical Techniques for K-12 Classrooms* (West Palm Beach, FL: Learning Sciences International).

PRACTICAL STRATEGIES

Dylan Wiliam emphasises the importance of establishing what learners already know and of seeking accurate evidence about their understanding as lessons unfold. These layers of information help a teacher to do two crucial things: first, plan for new learning to occur and, second, provide feedback to learners that is targeted precisely at moving them forward.

GOOD TEACHING STARTS FROM WHERE THE LEARNERS ARE

▓ Make a habit of establishing what the learners already know or can already do before you plan how to teach them. Once this baseline has been established you can compile a list of what the students need to learn in order to move forward. Using the pupils' own questions about their work can be useful here.

▓ Instead of using a simple test to establish current levels of understanding, try revealing pupils' thinking by having them generate their own test questions. This is likely to give you valuable insight into what you and they need to do next to improve their grasp of the topic.

FINDING OUT WHAT OUR STUDENTS ARE LEARNING

As Dylan Wiliam points out, it is important to acknowledge that what we have taught pupils is not necessarily the same as what they have learned! Try some of the following ideas for seeking feedback about the impact of your teaching during the lesson itself.

■ Instead of eliciting answers from one pupil at a time or assessing only the learning needs of those who volunteer, use one of these techniques to seek feedback from and require involvement from every member of a class:

> Ask the learners to write their answers on mini whiteboards and hold them up for your scrutiny.

> Ask the learners to hold up lettered cards to indicate their selected answer to multiple choice questions. You might even like to use an iOS or Android app that allows you to scan the room with your own smartphone – recognising the cards, and capturing and recording the particular answers that the students choose.

> Once you have posed a probing question to the whole class, give the pupils time to rehearse a possible answer with a classmate and then use a random name generator to select which pupil will share their answer to the question. (These can be found online or

you could use a manual process such as a bingo ball machine or drawing names from a hat.) This technique reinforces the need for every pupil to reflect and prepare a contribution.

■ Listen carefully to the answers the learners give to see what else you can glean about their level of understanding beyond whether or not they knew the correct answer. For example, if you ask the question, 'Why does the word "can't" have an apostrophe in it?' and the pupil answers, 'Because it's a spilt diagram …' you can establish far more than simply the fact that the pupil doesn't understand contractions. For instance, they clearly still don't understand the meaning of 'split digraph' and they probably don't know what a diagram is either!

■ Avoid asking questions that allow the pupils to hit on the correct answer by sheer luck. Instead, ask questions which require the learners to explain their understanding. For example, instead of asking, 'Is "slippery, slimy snake" an example of alliteration?' ask, 'Why is that phrase an example of alliteration?'

■ To keep a careful eye on understanding while you are instructing the class, and to hold every learner accountable for providing you with constant feedback about their understanding, give each learner an item they can display on their desks to indicate whether they do or do not comprehend what is being taught. When a learner signals their confusion, select a learner who is still indicating that they are confidently grasping the content to answer the confused student's question.

PROVIDING FEEDBACK TO STUDENTS THAT HELPS THEM TO MOVE THEIR LEARNING FORWARD

Dylan Wiliam stresses that the purpose of giving feedback is to help a learner know how to make progress. If you're not going to require the learner to act on formative feedback, then why give it? A good rule to remember is that if you spend five minutes giving a learner suggestions for how to improve, then that learner should spend at least that amount of time making the improvements. Use the following strategies to make sure the learners engage with and use the feedback you give them.

- Instead of giving your feedback in the form of instructions, try presenting several questions about the work to which that learner must respond.

- Instead of correcting written work, tell the learner how many mistakes there are that need fixing and encourage them to identify and fix them independently.

- Highlight three things in green that successfully meet the objective and highlight one thing in red that needs improving. The learners must use this coding to identify what they have done well and what their target should be. Alternatively, all four observations about the learner's work can be highlighted in the same colour and it is up to the learner to work out which have met the objective and which one requires development.

■ Write your feedback about your pupils' work on sticky notes instead of directly on their pieces of work. Get the learners to work in groups to decide which piece of feedback was intended for which of their pieces of work.

ARTHUR L. COSTA is Professor Emeritus of Education at California State University, Sacramento, and co-founder of the Institute for Intelligent Behavior in El Dorado Hills, California. He has served as a classroom teacher, curriculum consultant, assistant superintendent for instruction and director of educational programmes for the National Aeronautics and Space Administration. He has devoted his career to improving education through more 'thought-full' instruction and assessment.

ROBERT J. GARMSTON is an Emeritus Professor of Educational Administration at California State University, Sacramento. Formerly a classroom teacher, principal, director of instruction and acting superintendent, he worked (until June 2016) as an educational consultant specialising in leadership, learning, and personal and organisational development. He is co-developer of two professional development programmes used in the United States and abroad: Cognitive Coaching and Adaptive Schools (www.thinkingcollaborative.com). He has made presentations and conducted workshops for teachers, administrators and staff developers throughout the United States as well as in Canada, Africa, Asia, Australia, Europe and the Middle East. He is the author of a number of books, some of which have been translated into Arabic, Dutch, Hebrew, Italian and Spanish.

CHAPTER 2

A FEEDBACK PERSPECTIVE

ARTHUR L. COSTA AND ROBERT J. GARMSTON

Feedback can be defined as a process in which a system regulates itself by monitoring its own output. It 'feeds back' part of its output to itself. The thermostat on an air conditioner is an example of an autonomous unit that monitors data from the environment and regulates itself.

When the goal is self-directed learning, certain feedback practices are counterproductive and some are useful. Self-directed learners seek feedback from themselves, the environment and others. They are on a continuous quest to improve. As Edward de Bono (2015) says, 'EBNE: Excellent, But Not Enough'. They are already excellent, but they know it is still not enough.

COUNTERPRODUCTIVE FEEDBACK

Evaluative feedback makes the smallest contribution to self-directed learning. It encourages dependencies and places authority outside oneself. Praise, in particular, shuts down thinking. As a result, the respondent may warm to the praise or, on the other hand, be critical of the comment because it is not relevant to the performer's goals. Evaluative feedback can shape behaviour but leads to low agency.

PRODUCTIVE FEEDBACK

Data descriptions without judgement or inference stimulate reflection, personal goal setting, self-monitoring and self-modifying thinking. The more specific the data – the more useful it is and the more it is in response to a perceived need – the more valuable it is. Feedback that is sought is most likely to be used. Developmentally appropriate data is also more likely to be used than data not targeted to the individual (Costa and Garmston, 2015).

Trust is a must. Relationships are responsible for 30% of the value in one-on-one relationships (Rock and Page, 2009) and trust is essential for transformational conversations (Glaser, 2014). In relationships valuing self-directed learning, the performer needs to know – even better choose – what data is to be collected by an observer and how, and the context and timing for the observation and subsequent conversation. They also need to be assured that the person providing feedback withholds judgement and inference. Ideally a person observed would have a conversation with the observer prior to the performance and inform the observer of the performer's goals in the activity and what personal learning is desired.

Consistent with fostering self-directed learning is the use of meditational questions that invite the observed person to sharpen their recall skills, which are essential to self-analysis, and generalise learning from one setting to another. For example: what indicators let you know the class was interested in your topic? What learning will you carry forth to future projects?

TOWARDS THE HIGHER GOAL

The most effective feedback practices are congruent with the organisation's mission. Should your mission be to foster and develop habits of enquiry within students and staff or promote self-directed learning, these comments here are relevant. Use evaluative feedback if, instead, your goal is to bring uniformity to teaching practices.

FURTHER READING

Costa, Arthur and Garmston, Robert (2015). *Cognitive Coaching: Developing Self-Directed Leaders and Learners* (Lanham, MD: Rowman & Littlefield).

de Bono, Edward (2015). Presentation at the International Conference on Thinking (ICOT), Bilbao, Spain, 3 July.

Glaser, Judith (2014). *Conversational Intelligence: How Great Leaders Build Trust and Get Extraordinary Results* (Brookline, MA: Brookline Communications).

Rock, David and Page, Linda (2009). *Coaching With the Brain in Mind: Foundations for Practice* (Hoboken, NJ: Wiley).

PRACTICAL STRATEGIES

Developing a self-directed learning ethos in your classroom is an important step in moving feedback away from a top-down process, where the assessor's word is gospel and the assessed simply soak up the feedback and act upon it in the way they have been told. Art Costa and Robert Garmston introduce an alternative here – building habits, routines and practices that allow the learners to play a more active role in the feedback process, becoming seekers rather than simply receivers of feedback.

SEEKING FEEDBACK AND BUILDING TRUST

▨ Establish a routine of learners self-evaluating extended pieces of work with the core question being, 'What would I like you to notice about my work?' Before submitting their work and seeking feedback on their progress, they should think carefully about which elements they would most like your feedback on, allowing learners an opportunity to think carefully for themselves about what feedback they need most, rather than waiting for someone else to decide for them. Questions they might consider include:

> Is there an element of the success criteria that I feel I have been especially successful with?

> Was there an aspect of the task that I have felt less confident about, where focused feedback might be most useful?

> Have I been focusing on developing a particular skill or technique that has been showcased in the piece of work (perhaps that has previously been identified as an area for improvement)?

> Have I used any innovative resources or additional information I would like feedback on?

It's also worth noting that we should not ask learners to seek feedback on a piece of work (either from a peer or adult support) until they have had an opportunity to make it the very best that they can independently. Being forced to share partially completed or unedited work can make learners feel vulnerable in terms of the way their work will be viewed. By insisting their work is self-edited first, this will ensure that the feedback they receive points them in directions that they could not have discovered themselves and is key to them feeling confident about the work they are sharing.

■ Use the following principle with colleagues in your school to develop a self-directed learning ethos around lesson observations. Before the observation, the observer should ask the question, 'How can I observe your lesson in a way that will be most helpful to you?' Seeking feedback on specific aspects of their practice can help to reduce a teacher's nerves around observation and establish a greater sense of trust that the observation is for professional development, and not simply a judgement on their performance. This will also create a clearer focus for the feedback that ensues. Areas they might consider include:

> What questions would they like the observer to ask during the lesson? What questions would they like the observer to ask learners?

> Are there any learners/groups of learners they would like the observer to focus on?

> Are there any aspects of teaching and learning they have been focusing on developing (e.g. questioning, cross-curricular literacy, behaviour management)? Have they been on a course recently? Has there been whole-school training from which they have been utilising the principles?

> Do they have any specific areas of concern that they would like feedback on?

> Have they had any recent successes with the class that they would like the observer to keep in mind?

> Are they using any resources of particular interest?

> Are there any classroom routines/habits that the observer should be aware of?

MEDITATIONAL QUESTIONS TO SHAPE SELF-DIRECTED FEEDBACK

■ In both the formative stages of a piece of work and as a reflective, summative exercise, ask the learners to review their work with meditational questions. These questions should allow them to examine their own work carefully, seeking concrete evidence of the success and impact that their work has had in relation to the success criteria/ assessment objectives and also how it can be developed further. The language used in these questions should be open-ended and non-judgemental; it should stimulate thought rather than point towards a concrete solution. As a formative exercise, the learners will be able to use these questions to set negotiated next steps to improve their assignment. As a reflective, summative exercise, the learners can consider which skills they have honed and which still need further development. Examples of meditational questions are:

> Where might you see some evidence of [success criterion]?

> Where could [success criterion] be improved?

> What were some resources you used that were most helpful?

> What are some resources that you might use still further to gather more ideas/add clarity?

> What are the most important skills you have demonstrated in this piece of work?

> Which parts of this task might you want to review or redraft?

PROFESSOR BILL LUCAS is director of the Centre for Real-World Learning at the University of Winchester. An acknowledged thought-leader in education, Bill has been a school leader and the founder of two national educational charities. With Guy Claxton he created the Expansive Education Network for schools, the educational goals of which are reflected in their book, *Educating Ruby* (2015). As an author, often with Guy Claxton, he has written more than 40 widely trans-lated books which have sold more than half a million copies, including *Help Your Child to Succeed* (with Alistair Smith, 2002) and, for the BBC, *Happy Families: How To Make One, How To Keep One* (with Ste-phen Briers, 2006). Bill is in demand across the world as a researcher, speaker and facilitator.

CHAPTER 3

FEEDBACK OR FEEDFORWARD?

PROFESSOR BILL LUCAS

It's a truth universally acknowledged that a single learner in possession of a good teacher will not want for feedback, as Jane Austen might have said. For without feedback learning is just a series of random experiences. With it we can build on the past, learn from mistakes, adjust our plans and generally have a sense of the impact of our effort on our performance.

John Hattie and Helen Timperley have done much to help teachers understand the kinds of feedback which work. They describe three key questions which best shape the feedback process between teachers and students:

1. Where am I going?

2. How am I going?

3. Where to next?

At a micro level, Ron Berger has focused on the benefits of teaching students at an early age to give each other feedback in a process of group critique (see Chapter 7). In this way we can instil in them the benefits of learning from mistakes, of drafting and of critical friendship. I especially like his advice that students should always try to be kind, specific and helpful.

This kind of advice has served me well personally and could apply equally to situations where we are giving feedback to colleagues rather than to students. Here it is especially important, in addition, to give them the opportunity both to accept and reject our suggestions, especially, as is often the case, when we are doing it in front of others.

FURTHER READING

Claxton, Guy and Lucas, Bill (2015). *Educating Ruby: What Our Children Really Need to Learn* (Carmarthen: Crown House Publishing).

Hattie, John and Timperley, Helen (2007). The Power of Feedback, *Review of Educational Research* 77(1): 81–112.

Lucas, Bill, Spencer, Ellen and Claxton, Guy (2013). *Expansive Education: Teaching Learners for the Real World* (Melbourne: Australian Council for Educational Research).

PRACTICAL STRATEGIES

Bill Lucas very rightly tells us here that feedback – in all its guises, purposes and impacts – is the glue that holds our learning experiences together. He reminds us of two core points: that feedback should provide learners (tactfully!) with clear context and direction, and that choice and agency in feedback are powerful.

FEEDFORWARD – A STRATEGY FOR ROUTINELY ASKING FOR FEEDBACK

The following technique can be easily learned so that it becomes a habitual way of dealing with issues or problems.

1. Each teacher takes a moment to think of a work issue or problem that s/he is currently wrestling with.

2. Taking it in turns, a teacher describes a problem or issue in a single sentence, starting with the words: 'My

problem/issue is ...' S/he asks for advice from other members of the group.

3. Advice is given in the form: 'You might like to ...' (It is important to follow this precise wording if possible.)

4. After each suggestion the response is 'Thank you.'

5. When four or five pieces of advice have been presented, or when the group runs out of ideas, the process stops and it is someone else's turn.

Although the above example is framed around teachers' professional development, the feedforward cycle can be readily adapted to work in the classroom using guidance from teacher to learner or even from learner to learner.

ADJUSTING OUR PLANS

■ Consider the 'Where to next?' phase of feedback from a two-pronged approach:

1. What questions can I ask my learners to help take them even further? What additional challenges can I give?

2. How can I use the feedback I have received from my learners about their progress to tailor my teaching to best meet their needs?

■ The third step in the feedback cycle is more complex and requires us to look at the multidirectional nature of feedback. We are not simply providing feedback but also gathering feedback about our learners' progress, through observations about their work and their participation in learning activities, and using this to plan next steps both on an individual and whole-class level. Our lessons should never be planned, sequenced and paced simply according to our own instincts and preferences, but rather very specifically in response to feedback we have gathered from our learners about what they need and want most.

■ When marking a whole-class set of work, track the feedback you are providing so that you can easily spot trends in the mistakes and successes that your class have demonstrated. This can be done with a basic tally chart linked to the success criteria or assessment objectives that the work is being assessed against, or even simply by jotting a list of the gaps in knowledge, skills and understanding that emerge as you mark the set of work, adding a tick each time you spot the same mistake. Subsequent lessons, challenges and homework tasks can then be planned and delivered with these gaps and successes in mind, thereby 'feeding forward' with the feedback gleaned.

ACCEPTING AND REJECTING FEEDBACK

■ Develop an ethos of 'might like to' rather than 'must' in relation to the formative feedback provided. In order to retain agency and a sense of individual achievement about their work, learners should always be able to make the final decision about whether or not a proposed revision should be 'accepted' and carried out or 'rejected'. Learners need to feel empowered to make executive decisions about alterations to their work. Forcing change, especially where the learner does not agree that the change improves their work, will create negative feelings about the feedback process (even when feedback is provided in a kind, specific and helpful fashion). To avoid learners 'rejecting' suggestions out of complacency, create a system whereby learners need to justify their rejection, either clearly explaining why the work should stay in its original form or proposing a viable alternative revision.

■ Bill Lucas raises the sensitive issue of providing feedback in front of others and the importance of empowering learners to accept and reject feedback in this circumstance. When soliciting feedback publicly, be sure to gather a range of suggestions from the class. Once a suitable variety has been collected, ask the learner/group that has received the feedback to identify which piece of advice they will be most likely to action and why. To avoid hurt feelings in the acceptance/rejection of feedback, this can be done as a written rather than verbal exercise.

CHAPTER 4

FINDING TIME FOR FEEDBACK

DIANA LAUFENBERG

For the past two decades, DIANA LAUFENBERG has been a secondary social studies teacher in Wisconsin, Kansas, Arizona and Pennsylvania. She most recently taught at the Science Leadership Academy in Philadelphia, an enquiry-driven, project-based high school focused on modern learning. Her practice has deep roots in experiential education, taking students from the classroom to the real world and back again. Prior to her work in Philadelphia, she was an active member of the teaching community in Flagstaff, Arizona, where she was named Technology Teacher of the Year for Arizona and a member of the Governor's Master Teacher Corps. Her expertise has been recognised by earning National Board Certification.

Diana's 'How to Learn? From Mistakes' presentation has featured on TED.com, and her publications include a featured piece on the *New York Times* Learning blog, a co-authored chapter in an educational leadership book and an article in the *Journal of Adolescent and Adult Literacy*. In 2013, Diana partnered with Chris Lehmann to start Inquiry Schools, a non-profit organisation working to create and support learning environments that are enquiry driven, project based and utilise modern technology. She currently serves as the executive director and lead teacher for Inquiry Schools.

Feedback is essentially the mechanism for developing meaningful relationships around academic pursuits. This is a daunting task when you have more than 100 students to develop this type of relationship with. The 'why' is the easy part – knowing a student and their work is essential to helping them push themselves for more sophisticated educational pursuits. The 'how' is the daunting part, as the realities of a teacher's life become challenging throughout the year.

As a career professional educator, I was often challenged by having to provide frequent and meaningful feedback to more than 125 students in my classes. The overwhelming nature of that task is at times paralysing, but the potential impact on learning opportunities is such a motivator to continue to improve practice and method. Part of the process for me was to become more and more skilled at crafting a learning experience that provided windows of time for the students to be working independently or in groups. While that part of the learning opportunity was rolling, I would schedule short, focused check-ins with students to make sure they were on track with their project or task. In order for each of those check points to be focused and meaningful, I would often require students to fill out a contract for learning at the beginning of the project and then keep up with a graphic organiser as they progressed. These visual and succinct documents helped me to move from one student to the other with more ease.

At the end of the projects, I would sometimes schedule those check-ins again, and at this point the students would have already presented to their classmates, received peer feedback and then self-assessed their work. The teacher/student meeting was there to refine any of the pieces of feedback and to help hone the student's own ability to assess their work. The teacher contribution was about noting areas that did not receive comment or helping to better tune the process of evaluation.

If there wasn't time for a face-to-face meeting I would invoke another method of providing feedback on final student projects. I found recording oral feedback to be incredibly useful. There are a number of tools that allow for easy audio commenting on student work (I used Evernote). The workflow I employed was to gather all the evidence of learning: project, planning documents, contract, student self-assessment, peer assessment. Using this information, I would talk through my observations and then through the rating on the rubric, trying to be clear about the strengths and the areas for improvement. I found this version of feedback to be infinitely more clear and effective than written comments. From a 'use of time' meter, I leaned on this form of feedback instead of written feedback as I found the students were much clearer about the comments and evaluation.

Additionally, when I was teaching middle school for the better part of a decade in a technologically challenged school, we used folders and grade records to keep track of student progress. Each student would collect all the work from the week and keep a record of what we were up to throughout the week on a grade record. Each Friday the students would have a self-directed activity with newspapers (related to either history or geography) and I would have a meeting with each student to discuss their progress. This short window of consistent time to talk one-to-one with each child became a cornerstone of my teaching practice as it allowed such a good level of personal feedback about their learning path.

All of these methods take into account the challenge of just how daunting the amount of feedback that teachers are expected to provide is and the continuing struggle to provide that essential and meaningful level of feedback to the students.

FURTHER READING

Pahomov, Larissa (2014). What Meaningful Reflection On Student Work Can Do for Learning, *MindShift* (3 December). Available at: http://ww2.kqed.org/mindshift/2014/12/03/what-meaningful-reflection-on-student-work-can-do-for-learning/.

Stenger, Marianne (2014). 5 Research-Based Tips for Providing Students with Meaningful Feedback, *Edutopia* (6 August). Available at: https://www.edutopia.org/blog/tips-providing-students-meaningful-feedback-marianne-stenger.

Wiggins, Grant (2012). Seven Keys to Effective Feedback, *Feedback for Learning* 70(1): 10–16. Available at: http://www.ascd.org/publications/educational-leadership/sept12/vol70/num01/Seven-Keys-to-Effective-Feedback.aspx.

PRACTICAL STRATEGIES

MAKING THE AMOUNT OF FEEDBACK LESS DAUNTING

Utilising peers for providing feedback is a good strategy for making the workload of feedback less daunting. One strategy is to use 'speed learning' to facilitate unique and focused conversations between classmates. Students arrange themselves so that they are each sitting across from one other person. Use a visible countdown timer so they are able to manage their time well. Use a graphic organiser to focus the listener and facilitate active participation (see example on page 43 from the History of Anything project). Have the students switch three to five times depending on the desired outcome of the activity: less than three is not enough, more than five and they start to tire of the activity. Provide time for the students to process the questions they have heard and the feedback they have received.

HISTORY OF ANYTHING AND SPEED LEARNING

In each rectangle, write one fact each.
In each oval-tangle, write one question.

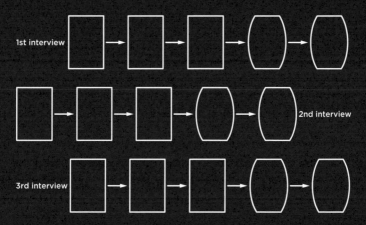

1st interview

2nd interview

3rd interview

▪ Try scheduling 'group debrief meetings'. By identifying which learners have targets in common, you can convene a special meeting with those individuals to provide feedback and development ideas which are tailored specifically to their identified need. This can significantly speed up the giving of bespoke feedback, while simultaneously helping the learners to feel part of a mini supportive community or 'special task force'.

MAKING THE MOST OF ORAL FEEDBACK

■ Follow up the recorded oral feedback with a short assignment that asks each student to draft actionable steps that they will take based on the feedback. They will share these with at least two to three classmates in order to make sure they have processed the information effectively and have a solid plan for the next steps.

CHAPTER 5

WRISTBAND PEER FEEDBACK

PAUL DIX

PAUL DIX is a speaker, author and notorious teacher-wrangler in huge demand. He is the CEO of Pivotal Education. As a teacher, leader and teacher trainer, Paul has been addressing the most difficult behaviour issues in the most challenging schools, referral units and colleges for the last 25 years. He has advised the Department for Education on teacher standards, given evidence to the Education Select Committee and worked extensively with the Ministry of Justice on behaviour and restraint in youth custody. Paul co-hosts the Pivotal Podcast, which provides free training to over 100,000 teachers worldwide every week.

In the early 1990s, all night dancing in fields was often accompanied with coloured paper wristbands. As a younger man I paid it no heed. Well, I was busy. These paper wristbands reappeared in my life some years later when taking my children to the swimming pool. In a moment of parenting and post-rave clarity, I realised that these wristbands would be much better deployed in the classroom. Perhaps those years were not wasted after all.

Integrating formative assessment into your lessons can be complicated, clunky and difficult to manage; bits of paper flying everywhere, technology not working, sticky note chaos. Cheap, coloured paper wristbands make the process simpler, more fun and allow learning to extend way beyond the single lesson.

Even in lessons when there are no books, desks, tables and chairs, success criteria can be recorded and shared. Peer assessment conversations between children are never lost; they are captured, worn and owned. Children literally 'wear their targets'! Somewhere in Westminster, in a darkened cupboard, a school inspector weeps with joy as his dreams finally become a reality.

Wristbands are really easy for children to record peer assessment conversations on. The bands can then be swapped, shared and returned. They are great for self-assessment 'on the run' and for holding key terminology and ideas. Each child can hold a record of their feedback and carry it with them to the next step of their learning.

The wristbands are not redundant at the end of the lesson. In fact, they become a fantastic way to extend and embed learning. Instead of just a plenary at the end of the lesson, the children will be re-explaining their learning to a range of different people throughout the day.

They will be questioned by other children: 'What's that on your wrist? What does it say?'; by other teachers walking around the school: 'Where did you get that from?'; by form tutors: 'Who is going to teach me something they learned today?'; and by parents around the dinner table: 'What has that strange man Mr Dix given you today?!' The plenary is taken out of the classroom and made real. Children have to explain their learning to people who weren't in the lesson, who don't understand the context and who ask challenging questions. As the learning is rehashed, re-explained and reworked in different places, it is embedded, deeply.

FURTHER READING

Dix, Paul (2010). *The Essential Guide to Classroom Assessment: Practical Skills for Teachers* (London: Longman).

Dix, Paul (2017). *When the Adults Change, Everything Changes: Seismic Shifts in School Behaviour* (Carmarthen: Independent Thinking Press).

PRACTICAL STRATEGIES

After hearing about paper wristbands, teachers have taken the idea and developed it to meet the needs of their own learners and the context of their teaching. Try some of the following.

- Wristbands as an exit ticket. At the end of the lesson nobody leaves without a wristband and declaring their targets to the teacher.

- Wristbands as an entry ticket to the next lesson. Bring three really big questions to the next lesson.

- Wristbands for planning. Children note down success criteria so they can be reminded of their 'direction of travel' while they are working.

- Wristbands to make connections. Make paper chains of connected ideas.

- Wristbands for teacher input. Prepare these at the beginning of the lesson with key teaching points/ terminology.

- Wristbands for self-reflection. Record responses to simple self-assessment routines: What did I give to the lesson? What did I take away? What trouble did I cause?

- Wristbands for behaviour. Children 'hold' their behavioural targets so they are subtle, private and easily recalled during the day.

- Wristbands to carry forward learning. Children hang up their wristbands on their own peg so they can easily transfer ideas from lesson to lesson across the weeks.

- Wristbands for communication. Urgent reminders, coursework, deadlines and 'don't forget' messages.

CHAPTER 6

THE SOUND OF SILENT TEARS OF PRIDE

TAYLOR MALI

TAYLOR MALI is one of the most well-known poets to have emerged from the poetry slam movement and one of the original poets from the HBO series *Def Poetry Jam*. A four-time National Poetry Slam champion and teacher advocate, he is the author of numerous collections of poetry, including *Bouquet of Red Flags* (2014) and *What Teachers Make: In Praise of the Greatest Job in the World* (2013). Taylor is a tenth-generation New Yorker and the founding curator of the long-running poetry series Page Meets Stage, 'where the Pulitzer Prize meets the poetry slam'.

 Before I say anything on the concept of feed-back, understand that feedback is nowhere near as important as *feedfront*, a word that doesn't exist because I just made it up. But if it were a word the definition would be 'spe-cific and useful information about a product or process provided *before* production starts'. In other words, clear expectations and directions. Nothing will make it easier for your students to work hard for you than letting them know exactly what you want them to do (even if one of those things is 'Surprise me'). If you feed*front* your assignments and pro-jects, your feed*back* will be much more effective.

But that's just semantics. Here's my real tip about feedback: *positive feedback is so much more effective than negative feedback that the ratio of the former to the latter should be at least two to one.* Especially when talking to parents! For every one phone call you make home – and you should set aside time to do this every week – to say, 'Your kid needs to work harder,' you should make at least two calls to say, 'Your son made an incredibly perceptive observation today!' or 'Your daughter reminds me why I chose to walk this path in the first place.' You will come to recognise and love the distinctive silence on the other end of the phone that means a mother or father is crying – crying simply because no one has ever before called home for a 'good' reason. It's a gratifying sound.

And you'll feel even better when those same kids come into your class the next day ready to work even harder for you.

FURTHER READING

Mali, Taylor (2013). *What Teachers Make: In Praise of the Greatest Job in the World* (New York: Putnam).

Mali, Taylor (2014). *Bouquet of Red Flags* (Austin, TX: Write Bloody Publishing).

www.taylormali.com

PRACTICAL STRATEGIES

Taylor Mali raises two discrete elements of best practice here. First, he reminds us that the best way to ensure we get the outcomes we are hoping for (or perhaps that exceed what we are hoping for) is to make our expectations crystal clear. Second, he delivers an emotive message about the power of the positive: feedback that celebrates success will not only reinforce the good work that has been done but also boost motivation and engagement.

ENGAGING WITH FEEDFRONT

■ Try some of the following ways to get learners to engage purposefully with the powerful 'feedfront' you provide:

> Share clear examples of the sort of work you are looking for in a gallery around the classroom. Give the learners a set amount of time to 'tour' the gallery, encouraging them to annotate the best features they have spotted on each. Help the learners to use these to work backwards to establish clear expectations and instructions about how to best approach the task.

> To check the depth of understanding your learners have about the expectations, ask the question, 'What makes a great one?' For example, if your class is

learning about writing a haiku, they should be able to tell you what features make a great haiku before embarking on writing one themselves. If they can't answer this question thoroughly, they probably should not be attempting the assignment yet.

POSITIVE FEEDBACK: STRIVING FOR TWO TO ONE

■ Set aside time to give positive feedback to pupils in a personal way by scheduling a weekly meeting with all learners that you feel have done something great that week. You don't need to raise the profile of this special celebratory gathering by offering a tangible reward; as Taylor Mali emphasises, it is the 'personal touch' – the teacher-to-learner contact time – that holds value.

■ What systems does your school have in place to flag up the noteworthy achievements of learners? Do they have a place on the school website to share achievements? Is there a 'best work' assembly? Do they send home a school newsletter? Are there school postcards to send home for learners who have impressed you? Conduct an audit of all the ways your school raises the profile of student achievements, both academic and extra-curricular. You may find that there are avenues in place that you are not utilising or in-house best practice that you could emulate and support as you strive to incorporate increased positive praise.

- Taylor Mali's suggestion about phoning home to praise your learners is an excellent one, and is sure not only to raise morale but also improve the likelihood of productive home-school communication in the future. At times, getting hold of busy parents by phone is challenging. To circumvent this problem, gather a class list of email addresses that parents can be reached at and use these as a means to share positive feedback. Sending a quick email to praise exceptional contributions may not have quite the same personal touch as a phone call, but it will be an effective, time sensitive way to open up those lines of communication, even for tough to reach parents. Challenge yourself to send at least one of these emails a day; it only takes a few minutes but is a great way to build positive relationships with your class and place a daily focus on positive feedback.

RON BERGER is chief academic officer for EL Education. EL guides a network of over 160 public schools in 30 US states, partnering with districts and charter boards to found public high schools in low income communities that send all graduates to college and helping to transform existing public schools (K-12 – primary and secondary) towards high student achievement, character and citizenship. EL's core work is in building teacher capacity through professional coaching, resources and open source curriculum.

Ron works closely with the Harvard Graduate School of Education, where he did his graduate work, and now teaches a course that uses exemplary student project work to illuminate academic standards. With Harvard colleague Steve Seidel he founded Models of Excellence: The Center for High-Quality Student Work, an open source collection of the nation's best K-12 student project work and writing. He is an Annenberg Foundation Teacher Scholar, and received the Autodesk Foundation National Teacher of the Year award. He is the author of *A Culture of Quality* (1996, 2011) and *An Ethic of Excellence* (2003), and recently, *Leaders of Their Own Learning* (with Leah Rugen and Libby Woodfin, 2014), *Transformational Literacy* (with Libby Woodfin, Suzanne Nathan Plaut and Cheryl Becker Dobbertin, 2014) and *Management in the Active Classroom* (with Dina Strasser and Libby Woodfin, 2015).

Ron was a public school teacher and master carpenter in rural Massachusetts for over 25 years. His writing and speaking centre on inspiring quality and character in students, specifically through project-based learning, original scientific and historical research, service learning and the infusion of arts. He works with the national character education movement to embed character values into the core of academic work.

CHAPTER 7

CRITIQUE AND FEEDBACK

RON BERGER

I think it is useful to separate *critique lessons* – whole class or small group analysis of exemplary student work to build criteria for what good work in that format looks like – and *descriptive feedback* – guidance for individual students, by teachers or peers, on how to make their particular piece of work better. Both of these structures are essential.

Critique lessons give students a vision of what they are aiming for: what a high quality essay, geometric proof, physics lab report or historical research paper actually can be. It is important to choose compelling examples of student or professional work and analyse them in depth with students to create a list of concrete attributes of quality, using student language and ideas to shape that criteria list. Because most teachers use the same formats year after year in their teaching, it is great practice to save the best examples for future use.

Descriptive feedback gives students a clear idea of the next steps in improving their work. The feedback must be *kind*, *specific* and *helpful*. It is most useful to narrow the feedback to a discrete dimension of the work, one aspect of quality, so that the student knows exactly how to move forward. If the feedback is peer to peer, it is most effective if the students collectively create a shared vision of what quality in that dimension looks like (e.g. how well-chosen metaphors can improve writing) and then analyse each other's work for that specific dimension (e.g.

Are strong metaphors used in the piece?), rather than simply reading a piece holistically and giving general feedback ('I like your paper – it's well written').

Whether the student work is centred on written literacy or maths/science literacy, the tendency for all of us – students and teachers – is to conflate conventions and accuracy (e.g. proper spelling/grammar, accurate computation) with ideas and composition. These should be critiqued separately, as they are typically done in real life: revision first, proofreading second.

FURTHER READING

Berger, Ron (2003). *An Ethic of Excellence: Building a Culture of Craftsmanship with Students* (Portsmouth, NH: Heinemann Educational Books).

Berger, Ron (1996, 2011). *A Culture of Quality: A Reflection on Practice* (Providence, RI: Annenberg Institute for School Reform).

Berger, Ron, Rugen, Leah and Woodfin, Libby (2014). *Leaders of Their Own Learning: Transforming Schools Through Student-Engaged Assessment* (San Francisco, CA: Jossey-Bass).

Berger, Ron, Woodfin, Libby, Plaut, Suzanne N. and Dobbertin, Cheryl B. (2014). *Transformational Literacy: Making the Common Core Shift with Work That Matters* (San Francisco, CA: Jossey-Bass).

PRACTICAL STRATEGIES

CRITIQUE LESSONS AND DESCRIPTIVE FEEDBACK

- As well as showing exemplary material, you can encourage active engagement with spotting best practice and co-creating success criteria by demonstrating how to do a piece of work badly. In this amusing activity, your learners' challenge is to spot what the 'bad practice' is and suggest how to rectify the mistakes. Careful questioning and possible exaggeration of errors can be the perfect way to highlight 'what makes a good one' from a different angle. This can also be an effective way to personalise the success criteria, as you use your 'bad' demonstration to highlight common mistakes that have emerged in the class's formative work.

- Room for choice and interpretation is vital for learners to think critically about the knowledge, skills and information you are sharing with them. For an exciting and interactive peer assessment activity, try placing a different sample piece of work on each group table with a larger piece of plain paper acting as a backing frame. Then ask groups of pupils to move systematically from table to table at intervals signalled by you. As they encounter each piece of their classmates' work, they must annotate it, making suggestions for improvements, alterations and additions. Each time they move to a new table, they should review the suggestions made by previous groups and consider how they can add further value to the feedback already given. This activity helps to emphasise the fact that work can rarely be considered perfect – it can almost always be revised and improved further (and further and further!).

WHAT IS KIND? WHAT IS SPECIFIC? WHAT IS HELPFUL?

■ When using peer-to-peer feedback, it is vital to take the time to explore the metacognition behind Ron Berger's important 'kind, specific and helpful' principle. His widely viewed video, 'Austin's Butterfly' (https://vimeo. com/38247060), is an excellent illustration of how learners can be coached to analyse each other's work and provide kind, specific and helpful suggestions for improvement.

■ Scaffold the feedback that learners provide to each other with aids such as sentence stems, checklists and key words for feedback that they should utilise in order to give advice that has a positive impact. You could also use the 'bad practice' example above as a means to deconstruct what makes feedback meaningful, allowing learners to see what might serve as a vague comment and what an actionable suggestion looks like.

CHAPTER 8

RECEIVING FEEDBACK

ANDY GRIFFITH

ANDY GRIFFITH is the co-creator of Outstanding Teaching Intervention (OTI) and is a director of MALIT Ltd. He has helped teachers and whole schools move up to Ofsted's outstanding grade by offering practical advice and getting teachers to try new ways of working with their students. Andy has won a national training award and has written and consulted for a number of organisations including the BBC and Comic Relief.

Here's the feedback icon from our book, *Teaching Backwards* (Griffith and Burns, 2014), drawn by one of our ex-students, Jane Strahan. When we asked her to design the icon, we described feedback as being about two things: the way it is given and the way it is received. She came up with this antenna icon which neatly encapsulates these two aspects of feedback. How you 'do' both sides of the feedback antenna will determine how successful you will be. Here let's focus on the receiving feedback side.

Not all students are good at receiving or taking feedback. Some can be too proud to listen, some lack the necessary interest, while others may dislike, mistrust or not respect the person giving the feedback. In these situations even the best advice/feedback will be wasted and the recipients will simply tune out.

So how can we get students to be more open to feedback? One way is through modelling. If we want students to be more open, then actively encouraging them to be honest with us about our teaching effectiveness is vital. When lots of students are comfortable saying to a teacher, 'I don't get it, Sir' or 'Can you explain that again, Miss?' it can demonstrate a positive classroom climate for receiving feedback. Confident, motivated students will naturally ask these questions, but to make this the norm for all students we have to create the space and permission for all of them to pose these challenges.

Another aspect of good modelling is showing our classes that we are genuinely learning from the feedback they are giving us. And it's important to tell the students how we are trying to adapt the way we are teaching. Teachers who do this become much more agile than those who assume the students understand or who just pay lip service to pupil surveys.

In seeking the feedback of our students through formal methods such as questioning and surveys, as well as informal ones such as conversations, we are demonstrating our humility. With this openness there does come the risk that there may be negative comments about us and our teaching. It is how we react to these comments that will demonstrate to our students whether we are more concerned with learning or preserving ego. And that's a great lesson for the students to learn from us.

FURTHER READING

Griffith, Andy and Burns, Mark (2012). *Engaging Learners* (Carmarthen: Crown House Publishing).

Griffith, Andy and Burns, Mark (2014). *Teaching Backwards* (Carmarthen: Crown House Publishing).

PRACTICAL STRATEGIES

SEEK FEEDBACK

■ Throughout the academic year, ask your class(es) to rate your teaching. Questionnaires, interviews and focus groups may reveal some useful learning points. Acting on some or all of this feedback, or explaining to the students why certain things are being done in a particular way, will demonstrate your openness. If your school runs pupil surveys, try to learn from them and take time to read the results. Be careful, though, on initial reading: some feedback from students can sting a bit. Don't react to it instantly – take a week or so to process it. Be careful not to ask the students for feedback and then indicate that you intend to ignore it or, even worse, that you resent it.

CONSIDER STUDENTS' HURDLES FOR RECEIVING FEEDBACK

■ Think about how your classroom norms can encourage students to be more open to receiving feedback. Peer marking agreements or contracts, where students sign a contract demonstrating the protocols they will maintain, can often be an effective strategy.

■ Some students aren't open to feedback because they fear what others will say. Getting the students to respect each other's differences can be very hard when they don't know each other. Where possible, create opportunities for the students to mix within groups, vary who they work with and share their interests with others. Ensure you celebrate people's differences.

■ Stress to the students that mistakes are our friends. It is through making mistakes that we learn to improve. Try to create a classroom climate where everyone is willing to share mistakes, the teacher included. This will particularly help those students who tend to be less confident to be more amenable. Being open to feedback won't guarantee that you receive useful feedback; you might actually learn nothing new. But you might just get that piece of knowledge that will really help you to be successful with a student that other teachers might struggle with. In opening that student up to feedback in your class, you might just enable them to look at themselves in a different, more positive way.

DON'T JUST ASSUME
LEARNERS UNDERSTAND

■ Think about getting regular feedback from your students in lessons so that you can adapt accordingly. For instance, try getting into the habit of devising and asking hinge point questions. These are posed by teachers at key points in the lesson in order to gather proof about which students are at the stage to confidently tackle the next challenge and which are not. These questions can be answered on mini whiteboards, for example, and give the teacher vital information as to whether s/he can move on or whether they need to do a bit of re-teaching (or pre-teaching) first. Multiple choice formats can be an effective way of asking hinge point questions without taking up too much time.

CHAPTER 9

PRAISE AND REWARDS:
DANGER – HANDLE WITH CARE
PROFESSOR BARRY HYMER

PROFESSOR BARRY HYMER is one of the country's foremost authorities on cultivating a growth mindset and a much in demand speaker who has worked closely with Carol Dweck on several UK mindset conference tours. He is interested in helping schools with practical ways to foster growth mindsets in their pupils.

Praise and rewards can work, but be careful what you wish for! There is an abundance of research evidence to indicate that they work at the cost of such precious educational virtues as intrinsic motivation and a love of learning for its own sake – from which independent learning, initiative, persistence at challenging tasks and the like all flow.

Praise and rewards (like stickers, smileys, tokens, merit points and certificates) are quick-hit extrinsic motivators that locate the point of learning as being the achievement of some material product. They are superficially attractive to many learners – and some learners come to be dependent on their daily 'hit'. But in their sneaky ways they keep you, the teacher, as the omniscient controller of someone else's learning and the learner as the passive recipient of your judgement and favour. Although apparently positive and benign, these extrinsic reinforcers are little symbols of manipulation, designed to ensure compliance or to compensate a child for doing something that their better selves might have chosen to do for other reasons, such as intrinsic motivation or even altruism. Incentives end up being an exercise in the administration of power. Intrinsic motivation to learn is the casualty.

The avoidance of slack praise does not denote a cold and cheerless classroom sterility. Don't confuse praise with its more hard-working cousins like acknowledgement, encouragement, recognition and feedback. Acknowledge the things that deserve acknowledgement (effort, risk taking, initiative, persistence, etc.), encourage further commitment and higher aspirations and, above all, provide informative feedback to guide future behaviour ('I notice that you've … but what would happen if you …?') rather than offering inert judgements about past performance ('This is really good work').

In a culture that has grown fat and complacent on quick wins and easy satisfactions, you might spread a little alarm and resentment in the early days of a praise-lite regime, but you'll win respect and achievement in the longer run. Easy triumph and unredeemable disaster are both unwelcome in the classroom, so treat those two imposters just the same.

FURTHER READING

Boyd, Pete, Hymer, Barry and Lockney, Karen (2015). *Learning Teaching: Becoming an Inspirational Teacher* (Northwich: Critical Publishing).

Hymer, Barry and Gershon, Mike (2015). *Growth Mindset Pocketbook* (Alresford: Teachers' Pocketbooks).

www.barryhymer.wordpress.com

PRACTICAL STRATEGIES

ACKNOWLEDGING THE THINGS THAT DESERVE ACKNOWLEDGEMENT

How do you create opportunities for purposeful peer-to-peer encouragement as well as raise the profile of those learning behaviours that deserve acknowledgement in your classroom? Try using a positive learning behaviour 'spotting' exercise to focus on the visible ways that your students participate in class. This can help to shift the value placed on product – a relatively transient achievement in learning – to more transferable learning, skills and behaviours that will enhance long-term success and progress.

- Assign to each member of the class one of their peers on whom they must 'spy' for specific learning behaviours that lesson. Be precise in the educational virtues you specify for scrutiny: do you want to encourage learners to ask more open-ended questions? Share resources effectively? Show perseverance or risk taking? Act upon advice/feedback? Build upon others' responses?

Taking as our focus some of the positive habits that Barry Hymer has highlighted here, a 'spotting card' might look something like this:

You are the 'spotter' for: _____	
Jot down some notes when you see them exhibit each of these habits.	
Effort	Initiative
Risk taking	Persistence

By placing an emphasis on particular behaviours, you will be creating better opportunities for focused feedback and observation of desirable actions to emulate. You could approach it from a 'bingo' perspective: once the student has observed their person exhibit all of the specified good learning habits (and jotted down notes about what they saw), they alert the teacher and debrief accordingly. The debrief can also be done in a 'guess who?' format – the spy shares details about their observations with the rest of the class and those classmates must work backwards to establish who was being observed.

AVOIDING SLACK PRAISE

- Be explicit with your class about the kinds of praise and feedback that are purposeful and those that are not. Co-create phrases and assessment principles to adhere to and those to avoid – your taboo principles. Create a buzzword and encourage your class to 'call out' those individuals, including you, who are not adhering to the principles when providing feedback (e.g. those offering blind praise or non-progress oriented criticism) and insist on a revision. Creating this paradigm shift may not be easy, but with the whole class on board and being critical in the way they provide and receive feedback, the long-term gains will be worthwhile.

DENOUNCING THE CULTURE OF QUICK WINS AND EASY TRIUMPHS

■ Language is a powerful tool: the terminology we use in the classroom can have a significant impact on the way that students view the classwork and their role as learners. Rather than telling a learner, 'You're really good at this!' emphasise the process that has led to the excellent outcome by pointing out instead that their hard work and determination have really paid off. Similarly, try banning the phrase, 'I've finished, Sir/Miss!' and instruct learners to ask themselves, 'Is this as good as it can possibly be?'

■ Avoid labelling pupils as 'talented' or 'gifted' as this undermines the effort that has resulted in an impressive outcome. Using terms like 'high achieving' or 'highly skilled' in schools, rather than 'high ability', reminds both pupils and teachers that understanding happens as a result of practice, commitment and opportunity; it is not an endowment randomly bestowed upon a lucky few.

PRECIOUS EDUCATIONAL VIRTUES

■ When the shift from praising product to praising process is underway, it is important to make explicit to our learners what an effective approach to learning looks like (in the same way that we provide success criteria for the work they undertake). What are the baseline learning behaviours we expect to see in our students that will best help them on their way? Rules associated with etiquette and conduct (e.g. raise your hand, ask before you get out of your seat, follow instructions, do not use poor language, do not shout out) are discussed regularly and in high profile ways, but how often do ideas about the learning process get explicit airtime? If we are seeking to weight our praise towards learner autonomy by rewarding effort, risk taking, initiative and persistence, then these words need to become part of how we acknowledge, encourage and recognise classroom conduct and etiquette.

JACKIE BEERE OBE worked as a newspaper journalist before starting a career in teaching and school leadership. She was awarded an OBE in 2002 for developing innovative learning programmes. Since 2006, she has been offering training in the latest strategies for learning, developing emotionally intelligent leadership and growth mindsets. She is the author of several bestselling books on teaching, learning and coaching, as well as being a qualified Master Practitioner in NLP.

CHAPTER 10

HOW CAN FAILURE HELP YOU GROW?

JACKIE BEERE OBE

Feedback is powerful – research has shown that good feedback improves student progress more than anything else (Higgins et al., 2014). It's obvious, isn't it? As a new focus for school improvement, marking policies are being rewritten to ensure that students respond to feedback. Many teachers have found that including DIRT (Dedicated Improvement and Reflection Time) (Beere, 2016) in their teaching at least provides space in the day to focus on responding to feedback and to develop a growth mindset that prioritises learning. But how can we ensure that our learners get into the habit of seeing mistakes as an opportunity and not as a threat?

'There is no such thing as failure – only feedback' is an underlying principle of neuro-linguistic programming (NLP) that I have used as a mantra since first researching resilience 40 years ago. It seems such a trite cliché which many may cynically smirk at, but to find perspective everyone needs to be able to step back from their initial emotional response and reflect. Metacognition (or 'thinking on purpose', as I call it) is the ability to stand back from your thinking and adjust the way you see things. This type of self-management has been shown to be powerful for learning, so having mantras that habitually click in when things go wrong can help us to turn around our thinking.

We need to work outside our comfort zones if we are going to progress our learning. That means struggling and making mistakes before we get it right. But when given constructive criticism to help us put right mistakes, our natural inclination is to feel slightly deflated; a feeling that can demotivate, lower self-confidence and be seen as a threat. The quicker we can reframe this, mobilise our inner voice to try again and enjoy the challenge, the more resilient we become. This resilience thinking that doesn't give up is most needed by the children who find learning hard and have to cope with getting it wrong – often.

So why are we so predisposed to the fear of failing? Natural selection favours the paranoid. Our ancestors who ran away from suspected (as well as real) threats were more likely to survive and procreate, so it isn't surprising that our brains can be over-protective when faced with a learning challenge. Even if it is only our ego that is threatened!

We all need to reframe critical feedback so that it pushes us to improve and not allow negative emotions, such as self-pity, to hijack any learning from mistakes. Resilient learners have a default setting which doggedly sees failure as feedback and to try again or use a different strategy. In this way, getting it wrong is a challenge to overcome, not a symptom of stupidity.

Thinking on purpose to frame failure as feedback helps us all to thrive. Everything that really made me stronger and wiser was learned when trying to pick up the pieces of a 'disaster' and finding a way to reframe it. Seek out critical feedback, then just get on with learning from your mistakes. And if you don't make any – you're not trying hard enough!

FURTHER READING

Beere, Jackie (2016). *The Perfect (Ofsted) Lesson*, rev. edn (Carmarthen: Independent Thinking Press).

Higgins, Steve, Katsipataki, Maria, Kokotsaki, Dimitra, Coleman, Robbie, Major, Lee Elliot and Coe, Rob (2014), *The Sutton Trust-Education Endowment Foundation Teaching and Learning Toolkit* (London: Education Endowment Foundation).

PRACTICAL STRATEGIES

Jackie Beere highlights two crucial issues here. First, she reminds us of the importance of ensuring that learners know *how* to respond to feedback in a useful, positive way. Second, we are asked to consider the fact that if it isn't 'framed' carefully, the feedback we give could have a negative emotional impact on the learner, which may ultimately be detrimental to their progress.

SEEING MISTAKES AS AN OPPORTUNITY AND NOT A THREAT

- Emphasise the value of learning from errors by celebrating a 'mistake of the week' or 'greatest mistake'. Model this, in the first instance, by publicising one of your own mistakes and showing learners how this helped you to make subsequent leaps forward in your understanding. When a learner is brave enough to try something new by volunteering an answer or attempting a task, even if they get it wrong, reward them by flagging up to the class how this courageous venture has actually helped to move the whole 'team' forward in their understanding. A classroom display designated for this purpose will help to commend individual acts of risk taking and effort.

■ When they are considering formative feedback from a teacher or peer, help learners to 'step back from their initial emotional response' by asking them to reflect on the following questions:

> Are there any parts of the feedback that I need to ask for more detail/clarification on?

> Have I acknowledged and celebrated the parts of the feedback that highlight my successes/efforts?

> What skill could I now deliberately and repeatedly practise to get even better?

> Can I rephrase the feedback in my own words, showing a clear understanding of what I need to do next?

> If I'm feeling unsure, can I share the feedback I've received with a classmate and ask them to help me consider what my next steps should be?

■ Give learners adequate time to process and reflect on feedback and to subsequently share with you any relevant information that they feel they need to. Establish a process by which learners can have a dialogue with you so that if they have had a negative emotional reaction to feedback, or they have misunderstood it, you are at least aware of this. If necessary, encourage learners to use sticky notes to respond to you directly about your written feedback, asking for clarification on things they don't understand, offering information or answers to questions you may have asked, or even simply sharing with you their anxieties about the feedback or their exciting subsequent breakthroughs.

REFRAMING CRITICAL FEEDBACK SO THAT IT PUSHES US TO IMPROVE

■ Once learners have received your feedback on their work, help them to see this assessed piece as their current personal best which they can now attempt to beat by heeding that feedback. In addition to helping the learners to aim for new targets regarding the content and quality of their work, it can also help to keep them positive by motivating them to beat quantity and time records. As you are circulating during independent work, agree with the learners the aspirational times by which they will complete a stage of the task or exhibit a new skill and note these down. Revisit the learners at exactly the agreed times to reinforce the challenge and celebrate their breakthroughs that have resulted from responding to feedback in a positive way.

■ Share stories with your class of people who achieved their goals by responding positively to constructive criticism. These might be examples from your own life or the lives of celebrities or sportspeople. You might even ask colleagues to share their stories with you and create a fascinating corridor display! It may be useful to use the example of sporting heroes who routinely review their performance, identify their mistakes, use their coach's feedback and endeavour to eliminate these mistakes in the future through precise, relentless practice. Open up a discussion about the futility of responding to feedback with denial, blame, personal affront, excuse making or, worst of all, despair.

CHAPTER 11

TARGET IMPLEMENTATION TIME

MIKE GERSHON

MIKE GERSHON is the author of more than 80 books and guides covering different areas of teaching and learning. His online teaching resources have been viewed and downloaded more than 3.5 million times by teachers in over 180 countries and territories. Mike has written a number of bestsellers, including on topics such as differentiation, questioning, growth mindsets and assessment for learning. You can find out more, and train with Mike online, at www.mikegershon.com and www.gershongrowthmindsets.com.

Feedback is effective, but only if students have the time and the means to implement it. Without this, the information given – whether it is written or verbal – will not lead to changes in student thinking. Nor will it lead to changes in their work.

Feedback needs to be thought of as a loop. The teacher elicits information about student knowledge and understanding, uses this information to frame their feedback, and then gives the students sufficient time and support to implement their targets.

At this point, the teacher is in a position to elicit new information – because student knowledge and understanding will have changed. Thus, the cycle continues.

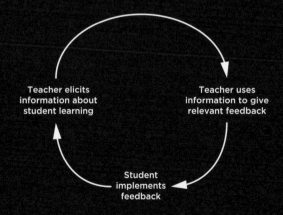

Teacher elicits information about student learning

Teacher uses information to give relevant feedback

Student implements feedback

Planning activities or lesson segments in which students can focus exclusively on implementing their targets is an excellent technique to adopt. It has three major benefits.

First, it helps you to remember to always provide students with sufficient time in which to work on their targets. By making this a part of your regular planning, you will habituate yourself into prioritising target implementation time.

Second, regular use of the technique will also create new habits in your students. They will come to see target implementation as the norm and will begin to think and act accordingly.

Third, you will be able to support students during the target implementation time. This means you will be able to show them how to implement their targets, giving them the models, scaffolding, advice and examples they need to be able to successfully improve their work and develop their understanding.

It is for these reasons that dedicated time in which to implement targets helps to make feedback as effective as possible, raising achievement and ensuring great progress.

FURTHER READING

Gershon, Mike. 'How to … Great Classroom Teaching' series. See http://mikegershon.com/books-and-publications/.

Gershon, Mike. 'Quick 50' series. See http://mikegershon.com/quick-50-series/.

Hymer, Barry and Gershon, Mike (2014). *Growth Mindset Pocketbook* (Alresford: Teachers' Pocketbooks).

www.mikegershon.com

PRACTICAL STRATEGIES

Time is the most common limiting factor for people when it comes to making meaningful changes and improvements in all areas of life. Mike Gershon has reminded us here that this is not limited to frazzled parents and busy professionals; if we expect our learners to make productive use of the feedback we provide, then time, coupled with high quality feedback, is the greatest tool we can give them.

MAKING USE OF THE INFORMATION YOU ELICIT

■ Use the knowledge gathered about learners' gaps in knowledge, information and skills to enable learners to collaborate in purposeful groups and pairings during the time you provide. Learners working together to close similar gaps or improve upon the same skills can support each other in up-levelling their work and meeting the challenging feedback targets you have set.

■ Use the feedback you have gathered about your learners' gaps to plan for a mini recap lesson before the target implementation time begins. This will ensure that all learners are clear about how to proceed once this time subsequently begins.

CHANGES IN THINKING, CHANGES IN WORK

- When you set aside time in class for learners to act on feedback and up-level their work, not all of the input and recommendations need to come directly from the teacher. As a homework task, ask the learners to critique their own work and create three actionable targets that they believe would improve the original piece. Remind the learners that the purpose of the homework task is *not* to perform the revisions but rather to analyse their work and set their own targets. Once the targets have been approved (and tweaked, where necessary) by the teacher, the learners can be provided with time in the lesson to act upon the agreed feedback.

- If you are planning on setting aside a substantial amount of class time to act upon targets and improve work, let your learners know in advance so they can prepare appropriately for it. Suggest to the learners some resources that may be of use to help them act on your feedback and create an expectation that they will equip themselves properly to make the best use of the session. If you ask them to source outside reading and research to enhance their work, setting some research questions to scaffold this may be helpful for some learners.

SUPPORTING LEARNERS IN TARGET IMPLEMENTATION TIME

■ The learners will desire and require different levels of support during target implementation time and it can feel very chaotic when there are hands up all over the classroom waiting for your attention or even queues of learners standing at your side for a 'quick question'. Try some of the following as means to manage on-demand support:

> Use a traffic light system for learners to signal when your support is required. Provide each learner (or group, where appropriate) with a green, amber and red card. If the learners are happy and confident with the work they are undertaking and do not require additional support, they should display their green card. If they have a question but it is not urgent, and they have purposeful work they can be undertaking while waiting, they should display their amber card. If their need is urgent and they need your support before they can undertake any further work, they should display their red card. At a glance around the classroom you can see where you need to intervene most urgently, without the need for multiple learners waiting around with their hands in the air (which is always an unproductive state!).

During his career, PROFESSOR MICK WATERS has been a teacher and head teacher as well as working at senior levels in Birmingham and Manchester local authorities. He is an Honorary Fellow of the College of Teachers and supports several educational causes. He is a patron of the Children's University, SAPERE and the Curriculum Foundation. Mick supports the National Association for Environmental Education as a vice-president and is also chair of the CoED Foundation which promotes compassionate education.

He has written books on the curriculum, teaching and learning, and leadership, as well as making presentations at numerous national and international conferences. Mick's most recent book, *Thinking Allowed On Schooling*, was published in 2013. He is passionate about the role of education in improving life chances for pupils and works with schools on raising standards and innovative approaches to learning.

> For the learners who are 'stuck' and waiting for your support before they can move to the next step, be sure to have a selection of best practice work (even better if it is annotated for key features) that they can peruse while waiting. This will make their wait time productive and focused on the task and may even provide them with ideas and techniques to un-stick themselves.

> Create a 'sign up for support' list on the board where learners who require your assistance can add their name and the question/need they would like your support with. Encourage the learners to periodically check the list and if one of their peers has asked a question/has a need that they know they can help with, they should do so.

CHAPTER 12

REWARD POINTS FOR TEACHERS

PROFESSOR MICK WATERS

Many secondary schools offer pupils incentives in the form of 'reward points' as recognition for effort, attitude or quality in work. The theory is that if there are rewards that can be accumulated, then pupils will develop delayed gratification as they seek the prizes available, as well as becoming the sort of model pupils that help schools and classes to function effectively.

The distribution of reward points also acts as feedback to pupils. But some schools find the whole process is counterproductive for the proportion of pupils who either receive few or are not driven by reward.

Try this for a variation: give each pupil 25 points to allocate weekly to the teachers who most help them to learn. The teachers receive reward points from pupils to cash in on defined benefits. Each week, ask the pupils to apportion the points between staff, with all points to one teacher, one point to each of 25 or any combination they wish. They can do this in person or electronically. Teachers get tangible feedback about their impact upon pupil learning.

The feedback might be heartening or dispiriting, as it often is for pupils. It might feel fair or unfair, as it often does for pupils. It might lead to questions of how to moderate the system to ensure better distribution and avoid all the problems of a perfunctory activity, as it does for many pupils. It might lead to rationalisation, justification and some resentment, as it does for pupils. It might lead to some staff playing the system and others rejecting it, as it does for pupils. It might work; why not try it?

Some will argue that pupils giving rewards to teachers would never work. So why might we expect it to work when teachers give such rewards to pupils?

FURTHER READING

Claxton, Guy (2008). *What's the Point of School? Rediscovering the Heart of Education* (Oxford: Oneworld).

Claxton, Guy and Lucas, Bill (2015). *Educating Ruby: What Our Children Really Need to Learn* (Carmarthen: Crown House Publishing).

Coyle, Daniel (2010). *The Talent Code: Greatness Isn't Born. It's Grown* (New York: Arrow).

Dweck, Carol (2008). *Mindset: The New Psychology of Success* (New York: Ballantine Books).

Griffith, Andy and Burns, Mark (2014). *Teaching Backwards* (Carmarthen: Crown House Publishing).

Waters, Mick (2013). *Thinking Allowed On Schooling* (Carmarthen: Independent Thinking Press).

PRACTICAL STRATEGIES

Mick Waters voices many of the uncomfortable feelings we might have around the efficacy of reward and feedback systems, and we certainly need to use our professional instincts about whether a system is purposeful and productive or whether it is a 'perfunctory' practice. Seeking feedback from students about your teaching can feel like a daunting prospect, but as Mick Waters points out, it can be an extremely useful practice for professional reflection – if we remain open to the possibility that we all have room for improvement! In addition to the strategy described above, you might like to try the following methods for obtaining useful feedback from the students about their experience of learning in your lessons.

■ Select five learners from your class to become a special 'board of consultants'. Take care to select a diverse mixture of learners who, between them, exhibit different types of attitude, background and attainment level. Tell this focus group that you need some feedback on their experience of the topic they've just studied so that you can improve the programme of work for a future class. To elicit useful responses, try asking them the following questions:

> Which parts of the topic did you find most interesting? Why?

> Which part did you find least interesting? How could I make it more interesting for another class?

> What aspects of the topic do you remember best? Why do you think that is?

> Which activities or tasks helped you to learn best?

> Which parts of the topic did you struggle to understand?

> Was there an aspect of the topic you wish we'd had more time to explore?

> If you were going to teach this topic to someone else, how would you do it?

You can use this strategy at the end of a whole academic year if you wish. Be sure to take the feedback you receive seriously and make use of it in a productive way.

■ What do pupils wish you knew about what it is like to be a pupil in your lessons? Ask them to write a private note to you in their books beginning with the phrase, 'I wish you knew the following things about my experience in your lessons ...' Next time you collect in their books, take care to acknowledge the message and show that you have considered it by responding with a note of your own. Remember that some learners will just enjoy this opportunity to let you know how positively your teaching affects them. This exercise will not only allow you to obtain useful information about the real way your lessons are experienced, but it will also encourage the pupils to do some meticulous self-reflection about themselves as learners.

- Share with the pupils an aspect of your teaching that you are trying to develop and ask them to help you work on it over the course of a week. For example, you might tell them that you are trying to make your explanations clearer, that you're hoping to ask more open-ended questions, that you're going to try not to rephrase what each student contributes, that you want to make your praise more specific or that you're going to try to encourage creative problem solving rather than rushing in with ready-made answers. Tell your learners that you would like them to keep an eye out (and congratulate you!) for your use of this skill and helpfully point out to you when you miss an opportunity to practise it. Sharing your intentions for professional development with your students can be extremely useful and it helps to build team spirit, not to mention modelling an excellent approach to learning.

CHAPTER 13

THE QUALITY LEARNING CYCLE:

FEEDBACK FOR SIGNIFICANT PROGRESS

GEOFF PETTY

GEOFF PETTY is the author of *Teaching Today* (5th edn, 2014), a best-selling teacher training text in the UK, and *Evidence-Based Teaching* (2nd edn, 2009), which summarises the extensive research on the best teaching methods, strategies and techniques. He has a reputation for explaining issues concerning learning and teaching in a down-to-earth but lively and inspiring way. His books have been translated into eight languages, including Chinese and Russian, and his ideas are used at a national level in Britain, Romania and Lithuania.

He has led more than 500 whole-day training sessions in colleges and schools, usually on the most effective teaching methods and on learning to learn. His website, www.geoffpetty.com, has lots of free downloads and is very popular all over the world. He is @geoffreypetty on Twitter.

When we learn, we encode the meaning of what we have learned in a little cluster of interconnected brain cells. This cluster of brain cells is called a 'construct'.

The new construct (shown in grey in the diagram on pages 110–111) is connected to what the learner already knew when they started learning (shown in white). This is rather as a dictionary explains an unfamiliar word, by describing its meaning with familiar words. Familiar is white in the diagram, unfamiliar is grey.

This construct is the learner's version of what they have learned; it will be incomplete and may contain some misconceptions. Careful feedback will improve the accuracy and depth of this construct.

Many, but not all, of the teaching methods that do best in rigorous trials follow the quality learning cycle depicted in the diagram. What is more, if we study reviews of research on cognitive psychology, we find it advocates that teachers set challenging tasks, get students learning from each other and ensure that both students and teachers act on feedback.

This is just what the high performance methods do. Also, researchers who have studied the teachers who make the most progress with their students find that these teachers do the same, and intuitively use a process similar to the quality learning cycle.

THE QUALITY LEARNING CYCLE

This diagram summarises why the best teaching methods work so well (see also Petty, 2009).

Set a challenging task

The task has a clear purpose and clear *success criteria*. It requires the learner to create their own understanding, linked to what they already know – their 'construct'.

This construct will have errors and omissions.

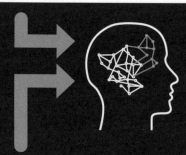

Improvement

The student, perhaps with the help of peers and/or the teacher, can now improve their construct.

The teacher can respond to errors and omissions in the understanding of the class and individuals.

Students improve their constructs.

Purpose of the lesson

Aims, objectives and other intentions.

The work shows the level of understanding

The learner expresses their understanding in their work on the task. ('Work' here means their verbal or written answer to a question, their graphic organiser, how they sort cards, etc.)

If the task is challenging and well-designed it will reveal the misconceptions and other errors in the student's construct.

The work is therefore a window into the student's understanding.

Feedback

The work gives feedback to:

- The student doing it (e.g. 'I don't understand this percentage bit').
- Peers (e.g. 'He thinks "mammal" means "human being"').
- The teacher (e.g. 'Quite a few students don't understand the concept of sensitivity').

We have good reason to believe that if teachers learn to use the high performance methods with understanding, the students will make much more progress. This is especially true if the methods you experiment with are focused on making good use of feedback gathered about weaknesses in students' learning or in your own teaching.

FURTHER READING

Black, Paul, Harrison, Chris, Lee, Clare, Marshall, Bethan and Wiliam, Dylan (2003). *Assessment For Learning: Putting It Into Practice* (Maidenhead: Open University Press).

Hattie, John A. (2009). *Visible Learning: A Synthesis of Over 800 Meta-Analyses Relating to Achievement* (London: Routledge).

Marzano, Robert, Pickering, Debra and Pollock, Jane (2001). *Classroom Instruction That Works*, 1st edn (Alexandria: ASCD).

Mitchell, David (2008). *What Really Works in Special and Inclusive Education* (London: Routledge).

Petty, Geoff (2009). *Evidence-Based Teaching: A Practical Approach*, 2nd edn (Oxford: Oxford University Press).

Petty, Geoff (2014). *Teaching Today: A Practical Guide*, 5th edn (Cheltenham: Nelson Thornes).

Westwood, Peter (2003). *Commonsense Methods for Children with Special Educational Needs*, 4th edn (London: RoutledgeFalmer).

www.geoffpetty.com

PRACTICAL STRATEGIES

GOOD TEACHING REQUIRES STUDENTS TO FORM A 'CONSTRUCT' AND THEN CORRECT IT USING SUPPORTIVE FEEDBACK

Let's look at the quality learning cycle being used in practice. Here is a teaching sequence that follows the cycle, adapted from the excellent *Assessment for Learning: Putting It Into Practice* (Black et al., 2003):

1. Warn students what is about to happen by describing the sequence below. Tell them there are, say, 12 key points that they must strive to get on their mind-map.

2. Explain the new material using your usual teaching methods.

3. Ask students to create a suitable mind-map to summarise the topic or an important aspect of it.

4. When their mind-map is nearly complete, ask the students to leave it on their desk and move around to look at everyone else's mind-map. The aim is to gather best practice from their peers in order to learn how to improve their own mind-map.

5. Students apply the ideas gathered while circulating to improve their own mind-maps.

6. Students self and/or peer assess their mind-maps. Provide clear assessment criteria for them to do this with – for example, you may share with the class the 12 key points that must, as a minimum, appear on their map.

7. Discuss common misunderstandings.

Notice that the learner must make a construct (personal under-standing) to create their mind-map. Also, when they look at their peers' mind-maps, they improve their own constructs. For example, a student might think: 'Oh, I had forgotten that' or 'That's a good way to describe it.'

The students then go through this same improvement pro-cess when they self or peer assess their mind-maps against the teacher's assessment criteria or exemplar mind-maps (see Petty, 2009 or 2014 for a full explanation).

The quality learning cycle is not anatomically correct, of course, but it is very diagrammatic and it does explain what happens when we learn.

CHAPTER 14

GETTING UNDERNEATH THE UNDERSTANDING AND ACTING ON IT

SHIRLEY CLARKE

SHIRLEY CLARKE began her career as a primary teacher, then a primary mathematics consultant, in the Inner London Education Authority. After a number of years at the Institute of Education, University of London, developing her interest in formative assessment, she became an independent consultant. Shirley is internationally known for taking the principles of formative assessment and encouraging teachers to experiment with ways in which they might be applied. Many thousands of teachers have worked with Shirley or read her books and, through them, the practice of formative assessment is continually evolving, developing and helping to transform children's lives.

Shirley's latest publications are *Outstanding Formative Assessment: Culture and Practice* (2014) and *Growth Mindset Lessons: Every Child a Learner* (with Katherine Muncaster, 2016). Her website, www.shirley-clarke-education.org, contains a video streaming platform of clips of teachers demonstrating formative assessment in action, as well as detailed feedback from her action research teams. In 2007, Shirley was awarded an honorary doctorate by the University of Greenwich.

We have known for some time that the more immediate the feedback, the better, and that the most significant feedback is the feedback the teacher gets from the child. Too often in the past we have discovered, too late, who has understood the learning in a lesson and who has not. Throughout a lesson we need to use a variety of techniques to help children reveal their misunderstandings and misconceptions, so that we can act accordingly. Unfortunately, it is often the case that we blame children for their lack of understanding or their task avoidance tactics, when the responsibility should always lie with the teacher.

Carol Dweck's (2006) work on the 'growth mindset' provides a wonderful message for children to believe that they can 'grow their own brains', and that revealing misunderstandings or mistakes will lead to feedback and therefore to further learning. Children should know that they are in competition with only themselves and that challenge is necessary for new learning to take place. Creating a culture in the classroom where transparency is expected takes time and is most effective when metacognition and the growth mindset is embedded in the school and is visible, tangible and referenced in every lesson.

Many factors influence the teacher's ability to get underneath the understanding as a lesson progresses: the classroom layout to aid frequent face-to-face questioning; mid-lesson learning stops to discuss 'where we are so far'; and whiteboards, traffic lights or written answers for children to show their thinking in an instant, to name but a few. Techniques aside, however, what matters most are children's and teachers' beliefs about their capacity to learn successfully. The 'Pygmalion effect' (Rosenthal and Jacobson, 1968) is the term used to describe the known impact of teacher expectation. In one of numerous studies, teachers were told that the lowest set was actually the highest set, resulting in atypically high performance. Children's confidence is profoundly affected by the way in which the teacher communicates.

A related factor in how children perceive themselves as learners is whether they are ability grouped. Thirty years of robust studies have proved that the more we group by ability, the lower pupil performance is overall. PISA studies have shown that the most successful countries do not group by ability, but rather provide more inclusive teaching (OECD, 2013). With ability grouping, the lowest group is typically given related but lower order learning, marginalising them from the skill being taught. For example, some learners might be making arrays while others are learning multiplication by the column method. Over time these learners are never directly taught those skills.

With random, weekly changing 'talk partners' as the framework for seating in the classroom, mixed ability flows naturally. If success criteria are co-constructed by teachers and children together, the children can follow either the compulsory steps or the possible ingredients in a task with partners – for instance sharing how they tackled a calculation against the criteria – and learning from one another. The most powerful resource for helping children who are 'stuck' or who need to be extended is another classmate. We need to be activating pupils themselves as learning resources for one another.

FURTHER READING

Clarke, Shirley (2014). *Outstanding Formative Assessment: Culture and Practice* (Abingdon: Hodder).

Dweck, Carol S. (2006). *Mindset: The New Psychology of Success* (New York: Random House).

Muncaster, Katherine and Clarke, Shirley (2016). *Growth Mindset Lessons: Every Child a Learner* (Abingdon: Rising Stars).

OECD (2013). *PISA 2012 Results.* Vol. IV: *What Makes Schools Successful? Resources, Policies and Practices* (Paris: Organisation for Economic Co-operation and Development Publishing).

Rosenthal, Robert and Jacobson, Lenore (1968). *Pygmalion in the Classroom* (New York: Holt, Rinehart & Winston).

www.shirleyclarke-education.org

PRACTICAL STRATEGIES

USING FEEDBACK TO REVEAL AND TACKLE MISUNDERSTANDINGS

1. Start lessons with a good question to reveal current understanding of the subject matter (e.g. Where did this classmate go wrong in this calculation? Where does the water go after it rains? This is a picture of the seaside – agree or disagree?) The plan can then be adapted according to responses.

2. Arrange the room in a U shape with rows in the middle if necessary, so that all learners can see the whiteboard but also talk to their partner. This arrangement allows the teacher to more easily walk around the room and speak to individuals throughout a lesson, asking questions which reveal their understanding.

3. Ask the learner how s/he is feeling. Learned helplessness will create a barrier no matter what you do. Combatting

this needs careful growth mindset strategies and never just sympathy (which only reinforces a sense of failure).

4. Display and reference a learning bullseye chart which has 'too easy' in the centre, 'challenge' in the middle zone and 'too hard' on the outside. Make it clear that new learning always starts in the challenge zone, but moves to the easy zone when learned. No learner should ever be in the panic zone.

5. Ask probing questions of individuals such as, 'So what are you going to put here? Why have you written this? What are you going to do now?' Then, when the learner answers, say, 'What do you mean by ...?' (Answers are often given without understanding.)

6. Randomise talk partners and when asking the class a question, give 30 seconds or more for partners to discuss their thinking before the learners are asked to respond. Eavesdrop where possible to hear the thinking.

7. Use mid-lesson visualiser stops in which one pupil's work is randomly chosen for all to analyse for successes and improvement needs. This models constant review and an improvement culture. It also helps the learners to unravel any misconceptions.

8. Pause the lesson at various intervals to give the learners an opportunity to tell their partner what they have

done so far, encouraging both self-correction and peer cooperation.

9. Ask a learner who has demonstrated good understanding to come to the front and talk through the task.

10. Pair learners who are still unclear on a concept with those who understand it well and ask for the expert to coach the partner, then the partner to reteach it back.

11. If there are more than four pupils who lack understanding after you have taught a concept, draw off that group and reteach in a different way.

12. Reteach the whole class if more than a third are stuck.

13. Where a significant portion of the class is struggling, reflect on whether it is the task itself which is causing the problem rather than the concept. Often the task assumes that the learners are further along than they really are or the task involves too many skills, obscuring the lesson focus.

14. End lessons with a five-minute summative task, such as an exit card, in which the learners are given one more example to complete or make one comment about what they have learned, revealing some of their thinking and understanding. (For example, after a lesson on guessing weight values, one child wrote: 'I have learned that a ton is the weight of a polar bear and can't be held in my hand!')

15. Teach all learners the same skill, in its simplest form, providing access to it for those who don't have basic skills (e.g. give times tables to pupils who don't know them yet so they can learn the procedure for long multiplication). Then offer differentiated challenges of the skill for individual follow-up.

SETH GODIN is the author of 18 books that have been bestsellers around the world and have been translated into more than 35 languages. He writes about the post-Industrial Revolution, the way ideas spread, marketing, quitting, leadership and, most of all, changing everything. You might be familiar with his books, *Purple Cow* (2003), *The Dip* (2007), *Tribes* (2008) and *Linchpin* (2010). His latest book, *What to Do When It's Your Turn* (2015) is now in its fifth printing. You can find it at yourturn.link.

In addition to his writing and speaking, Seth has founded several companies including Yoyodyne and Squidoo. His blog (which you can find by typing 'seth' into Google) is one of the most popular in the world. In 2013, Seth was inducted into the Direct Marketing Hall of Fame, one of three chosen for this annual honour.

CHAPTER 15

THE FOUR RULES OF PEER FEEDBACK

SETH GODIN

The first rule of great feedback is this: no one cares about your opinion.

What I want instead of your opinion is your analysis. It does me no good to hear you say, 'I'd never pick that product up.' You can add a great deal of value, though, if you say, 'That font seems hard to read. Is there a way to do a quick test to see if a different font works better for our audience?'

Analysis is a lot harder than opinion because everyone is entitled to his or her own taste (regardless of how skewed it might be). A faulty analysis, however, is easy to dismantle.

The second rule? Say the right thing at the right time.

While it may feel as if you're contributing something by making comments about currently trivial details, you're not. Instead, try to figure out what sort of feedback will have the most positive effect on the final outcome, and contribute it now.

The third rule? If you have something nice to say, please say it.

I've been working with someone for about a year, and in that entire time he's never once prefaced his feedback with, 'This was a really terrific piece of work,' or 'Wow! This is one of the best ideas I've heard in a while.' Pointing out the parts you liked best is much more than sugar-coating. Doing so serves several purposes.

First, it puts you on the same side of the table as me, making it more likely that your constructive criticism will actually be implemented. If you can start by seeing the project through my eyes, you're more likely to analyse (there's that word again) the situation in a way that helps me to reach my goals.

Additionally, it makes it so much more likely that I will come to you for feedback in the future. It's easy to interpret the absence of positive feedback as the absence of any sort of approval or enthusiasm. Finally, being nice to people is fun.

If I haven't intimidated you with my other rules, here's the last one: give me feedback, no matter what.

It doesn't matter if I ignored your feedback last time (maybe that's because you gave me your opinion, not an analysis). It doesn't matter if you're afraid your analysis might ultimately be a little shaky. It doesn't matter if you're the least confident person in the room. What matters is that you're smart; you understand something and your analysis (at the very least) could be the kernel of an idea that starts me down a totally different path.

FURTHER READING

Godin, Seth (2015). *What to Do When It's Your Turn (And It's Always Your Turn)* (Irvington, NY: Do You Zoom).

PRACTICAL STRATEGIES

Seth Godin's imperatives for giving feedback are especially pertinent to the subject of pupil-to-pupil feedback in a lesson. Peer assessment and feedback can often seem like a futile activity, with pupils offering opinions such as, 'I like your handwriting,' or focusing on insignificant minutiae instead of addressing crucial areas for improvement. The following strategies are rooted in Seth Godin's four tenets for feedback to help you make peer feedback as purposeful and useful as possible.

GIVE ANALYSIS, NOT OPINION

■ Explicitly teach your learners the difference between an evaluative comment and an analytical one. It may be helpful to show them film clips of feedback being given. These could be taken from competitive cooking TV programmes, sports commentaries or even corporate performance appraisal meetings. Encourage the learners to identify examples of personal opinion versus diagnostic advice. Which comments are vague and which are specific? Help the pupils to consider which sorts of comments are more useful and which are likely to be unsuccessful in moving the recipient closer to success.

AVOID FOCUSING UNHELPFULLY ON INSIGNIFICANT DETAIL

▓ Plan for peer feedback to happen at a point when it will be most useful in the drafting process. If the purpose is to generate ideas then it's best for this to happen early on, whereas feedback on grammar will be useful much later in the process. Before peer feedback commences, try asking each student to identify one area they would most like to receive feedback on. This could be an aspect of the work that the student knew they needed to focus on before they began the project or it might be the thing they most struggled with during the drafting process. The feedback giver must focus exclusively on this during their scrutiny and debrief of their findings.

▓ To help learners make sure that peer feedback is appropriate and pertinent, provide a checklist of success criteria for the task to act as a framework for the conversation. All peer discussion should centre around this checklist in order to ensure that feedback is helpful and relevant to the task's objectives.

RECOGNISE THE POSITIVES

▓ To ensure that positives are addressed and that feedback is given sensitively and received appropriately, try organising the learners into groups of three where one gives feedback, one receives the feedback and one observes the process and makes notes. This approach raises the pupils' awareness of their peer feedback behaviour. You might even ask the observer to provide feedback to the participants on the quality of their paired discussion!

▓ Seth Godin suggests that it is helpful for someone to feel that the feedback they receive is delivered by someone who 'sees the project through their eyes'. To help the learners achieve this sense of camaraderie, ask them to draft the required revisions together. In this way, there is a sense that the feedback giver is invested in the success of the project.

DON'T SHY AWAY FROM GIVING FEEDBACK

▓ Create an online sharing forum for learners to share ideas, questions and homework with their peers. Ensure that the rules for providing help and feedback are stated clearly on the site. This facility for online consultation will allow the pupils to access peer feedback as well as encourage them to review and practise giving feedback to multiple people.

▪ To encourage everyone to give and receive feedback, as well as focus on the importance of accuracy and efficacy, place large sheets of flipchart paper on each table. Each pupil should be randomly given a piece of their peers' work which they must place on the paper and draw an outline around. Once they have done this, they should write carefully placed feedback annotations around it on the flipchart paper. When this is complete, collect in the pieces of work (leaving the outlines surrounded by annotations on the flipchart paper). Now redistribute the pieces of work to their authors and ask the learners to peruse the feedback comments on each table, searching to see which of the annotated outlines their work must have fitted into. In this way, every pupil becomes a giver and receiver of feedback. As the receiver they must exhibit careful reconsideration of their own work and as the giver they are obliged to avoid vague comments for the process to work.

PHIL BEADLE knows a bit about bringing creative projects to fruit. His self-described 'renaissance dilettantism' is best summed up by *Mojo* magazine's description of him as a 'burnished voice soul man and left wing educationalist'. He is the author of ten books on a variety of subjects, including the acclaimed *Dancing About Architecture* (2011), described in *Brain Pickings* as 'a strong, pointed conceptual vision for the nature and origin of creativity'. As songwriter Philip Kane, his work has been described in *Uncut* magazine as having 'novelistic range and ambition' and in *Mojo* as having a 'rare ability to find romance in the dirt' along with 'bleakly literate lyricism'. He has won national awards for both teaching and broadcasting, was a columnist for the *Guardian* newspaper for nine years and has written for every British broadsheet newspaper, as well as the *Sydney Morning Herald*. Phil is also one of the most experienced, gifted and funny public speakers in the UK.

CHAPTER 16

SHUT UP, COACH!

PHIL BEADLE

The question I'm most often asked is about language. This oft asked question is related to the use of praise when engaging with small humans, and seems to reflect the view broadly embodied by the risibly titled book by right wing journo Melanie Phillips, *All Must Have Prizes*. The question, which generally comes in the form of a statement, is this: liberal praise of student achievement is an anti-intellectual sop that serves not only to give them a falsely elevated sense of their own abilities, but also proves that the people offering it up are liberal morons who do not properly instate orthodox views of authority in a manner that does not ensure our students grow (or shrink) into sufficiently compliant factory workers. Discuss. The view seems to be that praise gives students ideas above their abilities, dreams above their station, and that when everybody is somebody, nobody is anybody.

This view of the teacher who creates what a former colleague of mine described as a 'praise culture' makes the mistake of viewing praise as somehow pansy-ish, flower picking whimsy, and that teachers are prone to doling out rewards without either value or desert. This view seems linked to the right wing idea that a teacher's job is to enforce and uphold existing hierarchies. It is not. A teacher's job is to overturn them. The praise of our students, and specifically of the work they have done that is of value or has shown their development (from whatever starting point they were at), is vastly harder edged than the unthinking stereotype that it is somehow effeminate and sappy, that it wears a tasselled skirt and that no one ever won anything worth having as a consequence. Bollocks to specious non-ideas! Spotting the special thing about someone or about their work is a hard won, muscular, political and professional skill that comes with its own techniques, rules and language; and a transformational teacher will be fierce in their protection of it and of their students' right to receive what is, in fact, a basic human right – that of having a positive view of themselves.

Besides, what is its obverse? And does it work? To consider this, let me take you out onto a blowy football (or, grudgingly, soccer) pitch. Let's listen to the words of a coach trying to get the best out of a group of young players. It's a windy day. He's shouting, and negative expression is routine. 'Move the ball! MOVE THE BALL!' 'Messy, really messy.' 'NOT GOOD ENOUGH!' 'This ain't good enough.' 'Not good enough.' 'If you give him a bad one here, you'll do it on Saturday.' 'Get your levels up!' There is the same balance here of censure to praise that research revealed happens in American welfare families: seven words of censure (or wrongness) to one word of praise (Hart and Risley, 2003). And what is the effect? Does it motivate? Let's have a look at the science.

When undertaking a complex learning task we will have one of three goals:

1. Mastery – to get better at the skill.

2. Performance approach – to want to be seen as the best or as better than the others we are performing the task with.

3. Performance avoidance – to want to be seen as not being the worst.

The effect of these goal orientations on our ability to self-regulate (i.e. to control our own performance) is a matter of scientific fact. In a complex learning task performed with others, our goal orientation has a substantial effect on our ability to control our behaviour: mastery goals have an unambiguously positive effect; performance approach has an ambiguous effect, bordering on negative; performance avoidance has an unambiguously negative effect.

What then is going through the young player's mind when he is being shouted at? What is his motivation? What does he want? He wants the coach to stop shouting at him, to stop humiliating him. He is in performance avoidance. He fails to control his effort and focus, he fails to self-regulate, he stops learning! So it is with students in a classroom; if we want the best out of them, then we should make liberal use of focused praise about what is good about the work. We give them the right to a positive view of their own abilities. And then? And then? *Then* we tell them how to get better at it.

FURTHER READING

Hart, Betty and Risley, Todd R. (2003). The Early Catastrophe: The 30 Million Word Gap by Age 3, *American Educator* (spring): 4–9.

PRACTICAL STRATEGIES

SPOTTING THE SPECIAL THING

■ As Phil Beadle emphasises, it takes great professional skill to find a way to give learners a positive view of themselves when it's not possible to give praise for academic prowess or task completion. In those circumstances, you might like to motivate pupils by offering praise for one of the following alternative, and often underrated, achievements:

> Persevering when a task gets hard.

> Showing leadership qualities.

> Having a positive attitude to learning.

> Finding creative solutions.

> Working collaboratively.

> Taking ownership.

> Being well prepared for a lesson.

> Valuing other people's opinions.

> Helping a classmate.

> Accepting a challenge.

> Making a good choice.

> Trying an alternative approach.

> Reflecting on learning.

> Sharing an idea.

▨ Our approach to praise is not always entirely conscious. Film your teaching and review it carefully. Pay attention to the praise you give and use your analysis to inform your practice. What is the nature of the praise? Who do you give it to? When do you give it? Consider what you can learn from watching yourself in action. Are there any learners who rarely or never receive praise? Is your praise inadvertently biased towards a particular area of the classroom/a particular gender? Do you qualify your praise with descriptions? Do you use superlatives too easily? Are there any missed opportunities for praise?

▨ Make your praise specific. 'Well done!' is far less meaningful for a learner than when the praise is expanded to include a description of the success: 'You included reference to five of the techniques. Well done!'

GIVING PUPILS A POSITIVE VIEW OF THEIR OWN ABILITIES

▨ If possible, try to match your method of praise delivery to the student's preferred way of receiving it. Private praise, for example, can feel more meaningful for, and be more easily received by, older learners. Additionally, a one-on-one private conversation is likely to be remembered for a long time by a student. As an alternative to spoken praise, try secreting a congratulatory note inside learners' exercise books or surprise someone by sending a laudatory letter home to their parents.

■ For younger learners, you may wish to give praise in a high profile way. Try giving children a badge to wear featuring the words, 'Ask me what I did!' This badge, worn with pride, acts as an indicator to other teachers around the school that the wearer has received praise for an important achievement. The celebratory badge will ensure that the child is called upon to explain and relive their triumph multiple times throughout the school day and then again to parents or carers at home.

■ If you're praising a learner for successfully grasping a new skill or concept, you may wish to emphasise the commendation by asking that person to teach their newfound learning to a classmate. This offers significant recognition for the achievement and reinforces the sincerity of your praise, and the act of teaching the concept to classmates will highlight the pupil's own sense of what he or she has achieved and consolidate the learning that has taken place.

CHAPTER 17

NEXT STEPS ...

TEACHER DEVELOPMENT TRUST

The **TEACHER DEVELOPMENT TRUST (TDT)** is an independent charity, founded by teachers, dedicated to improving the educational outcomes of children by ensuring they experience the most effective learning. TDT seeks to raise awareness of the importance of professional development and building tools to help teachers to transform their practice and achieve success for all their pupils. TDT believes that demand for professional learning should be driven by the aspirations teachers have for the children they teach and the passion they bring to their work. TDT is determined to bring about radical improvement in the quality of the ongoing training that teachers receive based on the evidence of what creates effective learning.

Teaching has experienced a fundamental shift: we no longer see it as a delivery process, but as a *responsive* one. Being responsive means constantly checking students' understanding and adapting your teaching as a result; providing dynamic feedback turns a rigid lecture or one-way performance into a rich dialogue. This requires a constant flow of feedback from students, elicited by high quality assessment, coupled with individual and whole-class responses from the teacher.

However, as this book has demonstrated, without careful planning and execution, and the right systems in place, feedback can easily become mechanistic and shallow. The reduction of feedback in recent times into multi-coloured pen marking and verbal feedback stamps used in tokenistic ways has been a terrible diversion from the real purpose of feedback: to improve student outcomes. Through this book, we have also seen that teachers can adapt and develop their practice to engage in rich, responsive teaching, steeped in opportunities for expert and targeted feedback.

Research has found that feedback plays a fundamental role not only in improving student outcomes, but also in effective teacher development. The Teacher Development Trust (2015) commissioned an international review of the research into what types of training and development (also known as continuing professional development, CPD or just PD) actually help us to make the most difference in our provision. This is reinforced by England's *Standard for Teachers' Professional Development*

(Department for Education, 2016) which sets out the key ideas necessary for great professional learning.

Let's pull these ideas together and explore some ways to max-imise the potential for development and discovery that this book presents.

GETTING STARTED: PLAN AND ENGAGE

When you try out the ideas in this book, treat your trial as genu-ine action research. You will need to discover what works well, and does not work well, in your own context. It must marry up with the needs, aspirations and interests of both the students and staff in your setting, and be approached through careful experimentation, monitoring and evaluation.

The research suggests you need to design a sustained, respon-sive learning process (Teacher Development Trust, 2015) – that is, *not* one which is about learning and performing a check-list of practices or, conversely, engaging in prolonged pondering of only the theory. Teachers develop best when they pay close attention to the impact they are having on pupils, responding to feedback from the classroom to refine, challenge and build their knowledge and skill. This needs to be woven together with deep, professional thinking about why and how different approaches are working (or not working).

You will note how this responsive process of professional learning mirrors the effective learning of students in class. Designing opportunities for high quality feedback into lessons not only improves the experience for students, but it also gives vital diagnostic information for teachers to understand how effectively they themselves are developing, implementing and adapting new practices.

Key elements of this preparation and planning stage include:

- Finding time: identify and protect time for teachers to discuss and collaborate on the improvement of feedback.

- Prioritising and accommodating: work with a range of colleagues to identify which strategies in this book would be most useful in your context to implement and experiment with as a starting point.

- Expectation-raising: send small groups of staff to other schools where there has already been a lot of deep thinking about feedback. These should be schools that are further along the process of developing feedback and achieving aspirationally with a similar cohort of pupils in a similar context.

- Leading and selecting: identify which senior leader(s) will initiate and sustain the programme of staff development.

You should carefully consider which team of internal champions and experts they will work with and how they will negotiate with other leaders in order to find a way to keep the discoveries about feedback coherent with other school policies, plans and procedures.

All of these principles need to be embedded and sustained in order to ensure that the responsive learning process has the maximum impact. Many of these principles are exemplified in the 'School Leaders' columns within England's *Standard for Teachers' Professional Development* (Department for Education, 2016).

CARRYING OUT THE RESPONSIVE LEARNING

A great way to engage in professional learning is to begin with a pilot that involves an initial group of 'champions' who will start the work in the classroom. This should follow an enquiry model, where a small group of teachers collects evidence of how learners are currently responding to teaching, and then works through cycles of trying out new or refined approaches while continuing to assess impact.

1. **Diagnose.** Begin by getting group members to collect evidence from the classroom and present their findings at

a series of regular meetings. Collect pieces of class work, tests and homework from a designated period of time, along with lesson plans that identify the types of feedback used. Ask group members to pick a topic and record short audio or video clips (just a few minutes) of discussions with pupils, asking them about how they developed and fed back their learning about the topic. Get group members to go into each other's classrooms and focus on two or three pupils as they engage in learning. Your colleagues can observe how these pupils interact with other pupils and the teacher, considering how what they say, watch, hear and do affects their progress.

This phase is important to gain a deep understanding of the types of dialogue that permeate the classroom. You may be surprised at your findings, such as the amount of peer-to-peer feedback and how its quality varies. Gathering these observations also ensures that the whole process is rooted in real classroom issues – something that increases the likelihood of impact and success.

2. **Theorise.** In parallel with the diagnostic work, set a professional reading task for the participating teachers between the discussion meetings. Ask colleagues to read each chapter of this book and bring reflections on how it provides a new perspective, or perhaps enhances existing practice. In the group discussions, tease out how one chapter differs from another, what evidence it is based on

TEACHER DEVELOPMENT TRUST

and how it fits or contrasts with other chapters. The aims at this stage are:

> To encourage colleagues to start considering very different views and perspectives.

> To become aware of a variety of opinions and critically assess the evidence base of each.

> To use each expert's lens to examine current school practice and to try to contextualise the evidence that the group is collecting through their action research.

3. **Enquire.** Once sufficient diagnostic information has been gathered, it is now time to apply theoretical ideas. The group should identify one or two key issues that are barriers to better feedback, and prioritise one or two strategies that they think will help to overcome these barriers. It is important to engage in discussion about which are the most plausible, evidence based and most likely to be effective.

With your chosen focus and corresponding strategy in place, plan a lesson that one or more of the group will carry out in the near future, which both embeds opportunities for better feedback and gathers information about their effectiveness. Draw upon the evidence that you have collected from classrooms to identify:

> If the teaching strategy is successful. What evidence will you see that you have made an immediate difference? For example, how will essays, question answers, interviews and/or observations differ if the strategy is working?

> What evidence you can collect over time to check that this difference has been sustained.

> Which group of students you can use as a neutral comparison, to check whether it has been your intervention that has made the difference or whether these students may have made further progress without the chosen strategy.

4. **Repeat and refine**. In subsequent meetings, repeat the collection and presentation of evidence, exploration of strategies (with the underlying theory of why and how they are, or are not, working) and planning of refined teaching approaches.

Draw in support and challenge from expert practitioners, researchers and colleagues with varying perspectives. Use these colleagues to coach and challenge the group, to help you see ideas from different views, to solve problems and to ensure that your thinking is deepened all the way through the process.

5. **Present**. Once your pilot group has worked through key ideas, you can share these with staff through displays,

short TeachMeet style presentations, marketplace or 'speed-dating' events. These will provide an opportunity for staff beyond the focus group to be exposed to different presentations and afforded the opportunity to ask questions about the action research that has been undertaken. This can act as a spark for a second, wider round of research as you extend the work to a larger proportion of the staff team.

This process reflects the necessity of the ongoing relationship between focused action research by teachers to develop their own practice, the wider school environment and culture, and the use of outside expertise.

CONNECT AND SHARE

Both research and practical experience suggest that effective CPD is most powerful when an external facilitator is used to support key aims. This book is a really powerful starting point to begin exploring different perspectives. However, you don't want this stimulus to simply be a flash in the pan. To ensure that the ideas are properly explored and embedded, you need to consider how you can work with one or more experts in the area. In essence, teachers and leadership teams need expert feedback and constructive challenge just as much as students do.

Most of the experts found in this book are on Twitter and many have their own blogs. It may be worth contacting those that are most aligned with your own developmental areas to share some of your ideas and explore ways that you could work together. You could see whether they are speaking at conferences near you and prepare questions, or you could try to get them to come and speak to your staff team – perhaps via Skype or as a shared endeavour with a group of schools.

Another option is to explore which leading practitioners and academics are based in your area. Many universities will have academics who have studied assessment, pedagogy and learning and who are willing to work with teachers and schools – you could contact the faculty of education and/or the psychology department in the faculty of humanities at your chosen university.

You could also engage with relevant subject associations and specialist assessment organisations. This works just as well at primary school level, where most teachers are generalists, as it helps to connect them with rich subject-based expertise – something that our research suggests is central to high quality teacher development.

Experts can play a number of highly important roles. If possible, ask them to:

- Scrutinise the evidence that you are collecting from your classrooms.

- Suggest ways of collecting even better evidence.
- Signpost further reading and examples of schools to investigate.
- Model/demonstrate alternative approaches.
- Act as coaches and discussion facilitators.

FURTHER READING

Coe, Robert, Aloisi, Cesare, Higgins, Steve and Major, Lee Elliot (2014). *What Makes Great Teaching? Review of the Underpinning Research* (London: Sutton Trust). Available at: http://www.suttontrust.com/researcharchive/great-teaching/.

Department for Education (2016). *Standard for Teachers' Professional Development* (London: DfE). Available at: https://www.gov.uk/government/publications/standard-for-teachers-professional-development.

Teacher Development Trust (2015). *Developing Great Teaching: Lessons from the International Reviews Into Effective Professional Development* (London: Teacher Development Trust). Available at: http://TDTrust.org/about/dgt.

Timperley, Helen, Wilson, Aaron, Barrar, Heather and Fung, Irene (2007). *Teacher Professional Learning and Development: Best Evidence Synthesis Iteration (BES)* (Wellington: Ministry of Education). Available at: https://www.educationcounts.govt.nz/publications/series/2515/15341.

ALSO AVAILABLE

BEST OF THE BEST:
PROGRESS

UPCOMING TITLES
IN THIS SERIES

BEST OF THE BEST:
ENGAGEMENT

BEST OF THE BEST:
DIFFERENTIATION

World-class experts, important ideas, practical strategies

🐦 Follow the conversation at #BOTB

BEST OF THE BEST
PROGRESS

ISBN: 978-178583160-7

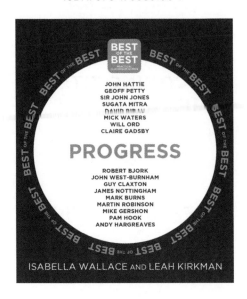

BEST OF THE BEST
ENGAGEMENT

ISBN: 978-178583247-5